Authored by Marianna Wetherill with additional contributions from Lacey Caywood, Casey Bakhsh, Valarie Carter, and Leah's Pantry. The authors thank the NOURISH-OK participants who shared their experiences, perspectives, and expertise that was used to develop this workbook. For a full list of resources used to develop these materials, please see references.

Development of these materials was supported by the National Institute of Diabetes and Digestive and Kidney Diseases of the National Institutes of Health under award number R01DK127464. The content is solely the responsibility of the authors and does not necessarily represent the official views of the National Institutes of Health.

v.04092024

Welcome!

What does it mean to nourish myself and those I care about? How does stress impact my ability to be healthy and what can I do about it? How can I find simple ways to practice good nutrition and feed myself in other ways that support my happiness and well-being?

Feeding ourselves can be both enjoyable and challenging. You are invited to spend the next 12 weeks on a journey to explore how food can make you more resilient, feel more connected, and express who you are. There are many exercises in this workbook to help you along this journey. Even if they may feel like they "aren't for you", we encourage you to try them anyway. To help inspire others, we also invite you to share more about how you are using this workbook through messages and photos at HowDoYouNourish.org.

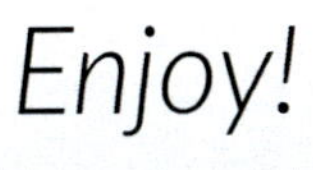

Scan here to visit HowDoYouNourish.org

Contents

INTRODUCTION

Important Safety Reminders

- Physical Safety
- Emotional Safety
- Food Drug Interactions
- Food Allergies and Intolerances

We've designed this book to help support your physical and mental wellbeing over the next 12 weeks and beyond. For any of life's journeys, your personal safety is always important!

We ask that you please keep the following in mind while embarking on this journey:

Physical safety

Although it's an important destination for finding good nutrition, kitchens can also be dangerous places. **Cuts** and **burns** are the two most common types of injuries that can happen in the kitchen.

Here are a few knife safety reminders:

- Keep knives sharp. More accidents happen with dull knives.
- Use the right sized knife for the job.
- Cut on a stable surface, like a cutting board.
- Cut round vegetables or fruits in half, then lay them flat side down on the cutting board to keep them from rolling while you finish cutting.
- Cut away from yourself and do not cut foods in your hand.
- Place knives away from the edge of the counter or cutting board where they might fall or flip.
- Avoid placing knives in a sink full of water or dishes. Immediately wash, dry, and store knives safely away instead.
- Store your knife safely by using a cover, knife block, or wrapping it in layers of newspaper or a dish cloth.

Use a chef knife for larger foods and a paring knife for smaller foods.

If you aren't comfortable handling knives, there are many healthy ingredients that don't need chopping such as frozen or dehydrated vegetables, ready-to-eat fresh or frozen fruits like berries, or pre-washed baby spinach.

Steam, hot pots and pans, and hot liquids can all cause burns. Here are a few safety reminders:

- If you have peripheral neuropathy (loss of feeling) in your hands, it can be hard to tell if something is too hot to handle. Always keep a potholder handy and use it when handling anything that might be hot.
- To avoid steam burns, remove the lid or foil away from you.
- Turn the handles of pots and pans inward while cooking.
- When cooking in a microwave, use containers that are microwave-safe and double check that there is no metal packaging with the food container, such as food inside a stapled bag or tin foil.

Turn the handles of pots and pans inward while cooking.

To avoid falls or spills, remove any slippery rugs or tripping hazards (possibly including pets and small children!) from your kitchen area before cooking.

Don't leave food unattended while cooking. If you tend to forget things or are distracted easily, set a timer or reminder on your phone to check on your food when using the oven or the stove.

Emotional safety

- The NOURISH program hopes to support everyone's relationship with food in positive ways. But, everyone's history with food is personal. Food, cooking, and some of the exercises in this workbook may bring up a mixture of positive and negative emotions.
- **If you become distressed, please take a break from the materials and use any of the mindfulness exercises at the back of this book.** If you need to talk to someone about how you are feeling, you can **call 988 to reach Oklahoma's Mental Health Lifeline** at any time (day or night). Next, please reach out to the NOURISH team so that we can connect with you with other free resources that are available for NOURISH participants.

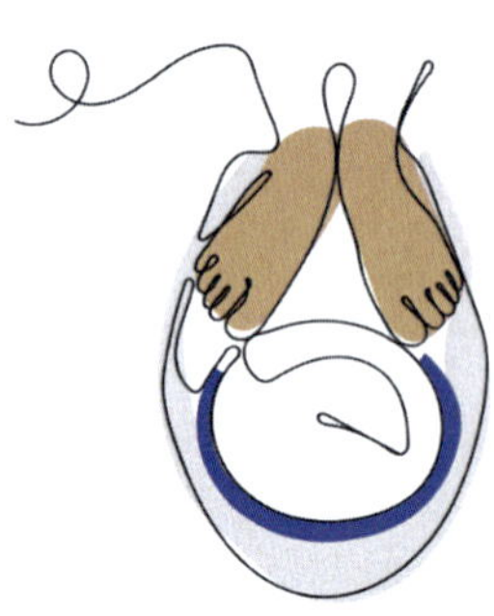

- Eating disorders can impact people of all genders, ages, races, religions, ethnicities, sexual orientations, gender identities, body shapes, and weights. This workbook is designed to help support people's relationship with food, but it is not designed specifically for people with a history of eating disorders.
- **For free emotional support and referrals for help with an eating disorder**, you can call the National Association of Anorexia and Associated Disorders (ANAD) Helpline at: 1 (888)-375-7767 or visit the National Eating Disorders Association (NEDA) website for a listing of helpful resources at: www.NationalEatingDisorders.org.

Food drug interactions

- Oral medications are digested and absorbed through the same pathways as the foods we eat. A food-drug interaction happens when a medication's ability to work is affected by food. Many medications need to be taken with food so they can be absorbed better or to help reduce medication side effects. However, for some medications, taking them with certain foods (or sometimes any food) can prevent their absorption or safe processing within the body.
- For example, many over-the-counter health food supplements, such as **extracts or concentrates** of garlic, ginger, green tea, cinnamon, or dark green foods, as well as supplemental iron and calcium, can keep some meds from being absorbed or working properly.
- The NOURISH food boxes will include garlic, ginger, green tea, cinnamon, and dehydrated spinach in a whole food (non-extract) form. Usually these foods can be enjoyed safely by most people when eaten in a standard serving size in their whole food form. However, when these foods are eaten in large amounts or concentrated and taken as capsules or food extracts, there is a greater chance the compounds in these foods will interact with certain prescription meds.

> If you have been told by your doctor or pharmacist to avoid any of the food items that arrive in your NOURISH box, or if you feel you might be allergic to a food that you receive, please do not eat it and let the study team know. Share it with a family member, neighbor or friend instead.

- If you are taking the blood thinner coumadin (warfarin), please check with your doctor or pharmacist before adding any green tea or dehydrated spinach to your diet because these foods contain vitamin K.
- **To know whether any of the meds you take has a food-drug interaction, please look at the package insert that comes with your meds and talk to your doctor or pharmacist.**

Food allergies and intolerances

- The NOURISH food boxes will provide many foods that are high in fiber. Fiber is an important source of nutrition for the healthy bacteria that lives in the gut (microbiome). As your microbiome begins to "wake up", bloating and gas can be a common and temporary side effect of eating more dietary fiber. To reduce fiber's unpleasant side effects, start with eating high fiber foods in smaller amounts, drink plenty of water with your meals, and you can try taking Beano® with meals if needed.
- Around 1 in 10 adults have some type of food allergy. The NOURISH food boxes will contain foods with common allergens including nuts, wheat, gluten, soy, and fish. If you have a food allergy, the NOURISH team will attempt to send items without your allergen(s) in your food box. **However, we ask that you always double-check food labels if you have a food allergy.**

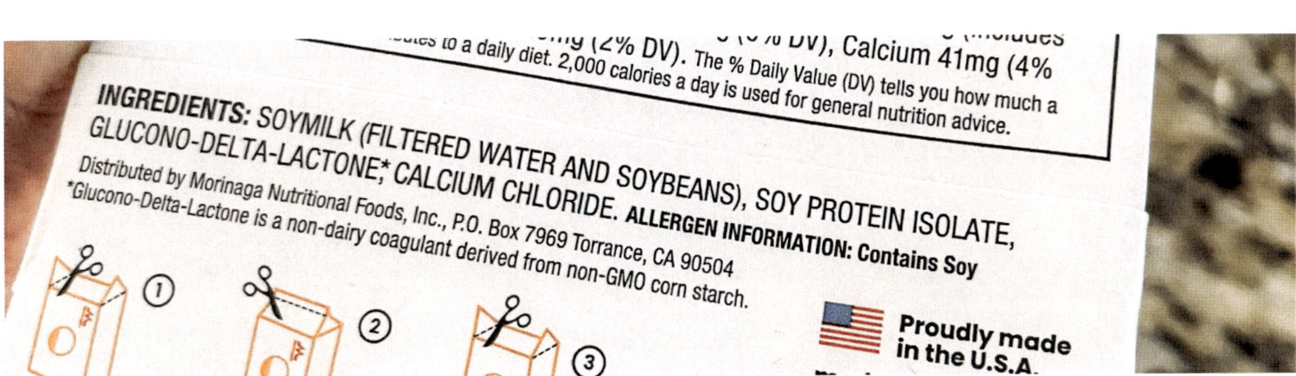

MONTH 1: STRESS MANAGEMENT AND MIND BODY CONNECTION

In this section, you are invited to explore:

- How food is part of the human experience and can be used to celebrate who I am as an individual
- How food, mood, and energy are related
- How food can help me manage stress
- How to create simple, balanced meals that support my mind-body health
- How to create a kitchen environment that makes cooking more enjoyable

WEEK 1:
Exploring the Meaning of Food in My Life

We are all worthy of happiness.

Roots of happiness

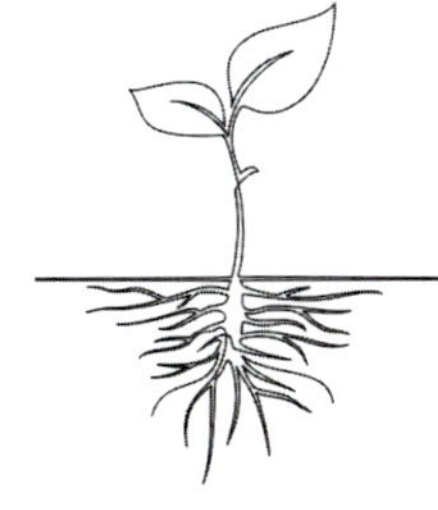

Every person has basic needs for survival. These needs include **food**, **water**, **warmth**, **rest**, and **safety**. Beyond these basic needs, there are other needs that are important for bringing happiness to our lives. These needs include **belongingness**, **love**, **self-worth**, and **self-fulfillment** (becoming the person we want to be).

What does food have to do with happiness?

Food and water are basic needs because our bodies cannot survive without them. But, food can also help us with discovering new ways to increase happiness in our lives. For example, mealtimes are a chance to spend time with people we care about, creatively express ourselves with new foods or recipes, support our health, deepen our spirituality, or strengthen our connections with nature.

When we choose to use food to feed one or more of these deeper needs, we also feed opportunities for happiness.

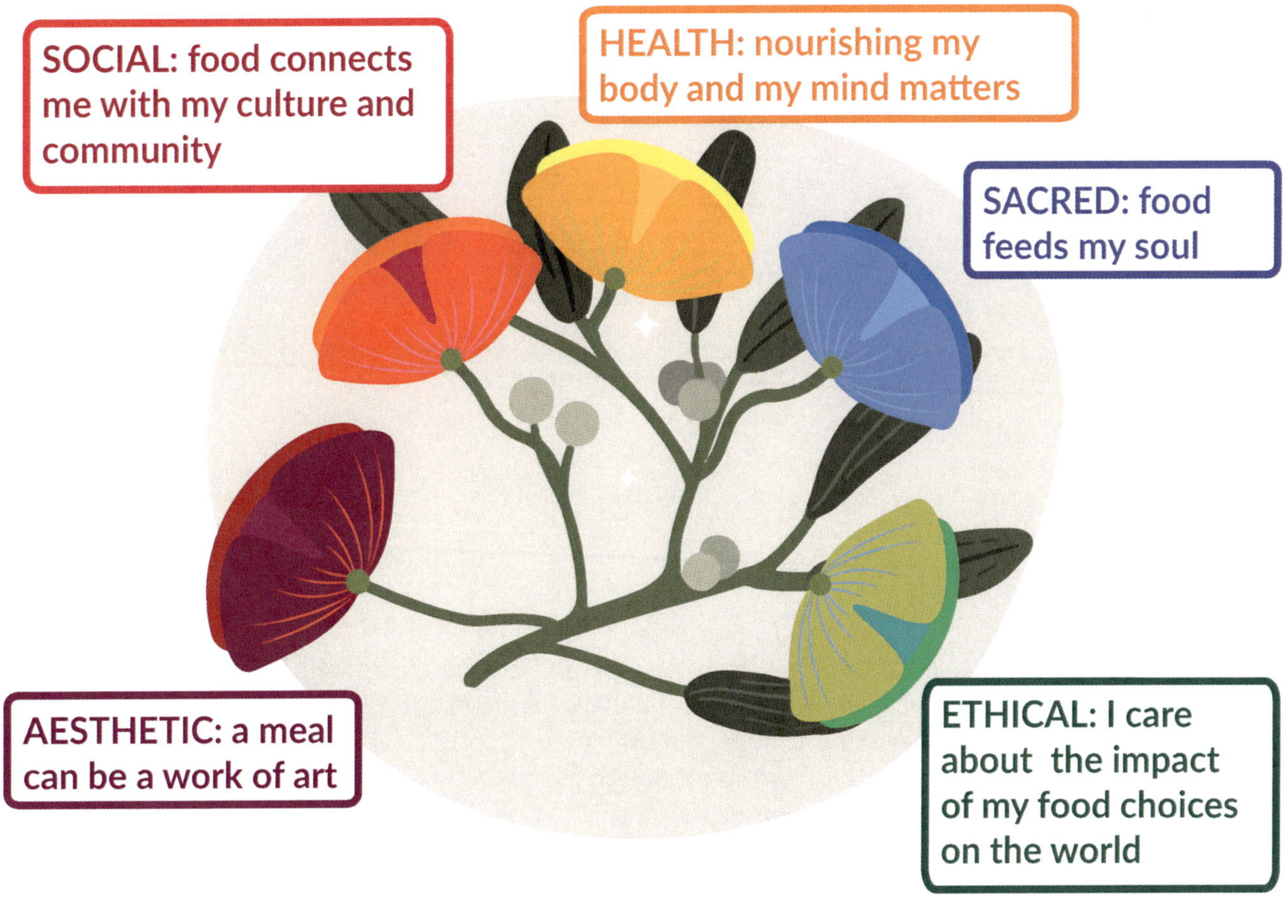

SOCIAL: food connects me with my culture and community

HEALTH: nourishing my body and my mind matters

SACRED: food feeds my soul

AESTHETIC: a meal can be a work of art

ETHICAL: I care about the impact of my food choices on the world

Your "Meaning of Food in Life" survey results

The Meaning of Food in Life survey is designed to help people understand their relationship with food. For some people, this survey can be difficult to take because it asks questions that they never thought about. And that's ok—most people are not as connected to their food choices as they can be. There is not a "right" or a "wrong" survey result. Instead, consider using your results as a starting place for discovery in finding new ways to nourish yourself.

Reflection: Meaning of Food in Life

When you enrolled in the NOURISH program, you completed the "Meaning of Food in Life" survey. Without any judgment, open and review your personal survey results. After you are done reviewing your results, answer the questions below. Remember, these pages are just for you and you do not need to share them with anyone unless you want to.

Have you thought about food in these ways before? What parts of your results are surprising to you? Which food in life meanings do you want to explore more? Why?

Special Note

What does food have to do with suffering? As social beings, food can foster happiness in many ways. But, for many of us, food can also be a source of unhappiness or suffering. For example, food suffering can stem from unpleasant childhood food memories or feeling deprived when we can't eat or serve others the kinds of foods we want due to cost, health, or other reasons. Please see the emotional safety section in this book for more information on helpful resources.

Food can be used to positively or negatively cope with other causes of unhappiness or stress in our lives. We will explore more about the relationships between food and mental health in Week 3.

Activity: Which Meanings Can You Find?

Below are several quotes from different people in the community when they were asked to describe their relationship with food.

Can you find at least one Meaning of Food in Life in each quote? Are there any quotes where you see multiple meanings? Do you relate to any of these quotes?

"My relationship with food is love. When you feed somebody, it's like showing them love. My relationship with food also connects me to Mother Earth. She provides all the food we need, so it's a strong, very important relationship really."

____

"I didn't realize until recently about how much food could be and should be natural."

____

"As I've grown, I've put more emphasis on fresh fruits from fresh sources with low additives or low pesticides. If I have the option of selecting something that is organic versus non-organic or that is fresher, I will make those choices if I can."

____

"Food is medicine because food feeds us beyond a physical level–it feeds us emotionally and mentally, as well. From all the hands that touch the food to when they get to your hands and how they were grown and how they were cultivated, all those energies play a part into how it is a resource for your body."

____

"I get all my food from a pantry, so it's kind of an activity for me now to make meals that I enjoy based on what's available to me. I can't work, and now I am learning to make new foods at home. I've learned how to make French baguettes, cakes, and cookies. When I get different baking mixes, I sometimes add different spices, like some African ginger, or nutmeg, or instead of eggs I might use Greek yogurt, so it's fun. It's an activity, it's a hobby now. And I just share it with my friends, and they like it."

____

"Food brings me satisfaction, community, and a feeling of family."

____

Aesthetic: How can I use food to creatively **express myself or appreciate beauty?**

Social: How can my food choices help me to **find or foster relationships with others in my past, present, and future?**

Health: How can my food choices help to nourish my **mental and physical well-being?**

Sacred: How can I use food to connect with the **sacred or spiritual world?**

Ethical: How can my food choices make the world **a better place for society, animals, or the environment?**

TRY IT! CONNECTING FOOD WITH MY LIFE VALUES

Food can help us discover happiness in new and meaningful ways

Which food in life meaning(s) would I like to nourish within myself and other people I care about in my life? Which would I like to explore more, but still aren't quite sure about?

Try It! Here are a few options for actions you can take over the next 12 weeks to strengthen each type of food in life meaning. Consider trying at least one new option from each life meaning.

Aesthetic: How can I use food to **creatively express myself or appreciate beauty?**

- ☐ Practice eating with the five senses (sight, taste, touch, smell, sound of food) at mealtimes.
- ☐ Experiment with new spices or herbs to create my own unique dishes.
- ☐ Add a pop of color using vegetables or fruits to everyday foods.
- ☐ Learn new knife skills to create more visually-appealing dishes, such as chiffonade, julienne, bias cut, and wedges.
- ☐ Something else: ______________________________

Social: How can my food choices help me to **find or foster relationships** with others in my past, present, and future?

- ☐ Sharing or making a new recipe with a friend, partner, or family.
- ☐ Making a recipe passed down by a family member or friend who has passed to honor their memory.
- ☐ Explore traditional foods from my family's country or countries of origin.
- ☐ Eating a meal with someone I care about (pets included!).
- ☐ Something else: ______________________________

Health: How can my food choices help to nourish my **mental and physical well-being?**

- ☐ Create meals that provide a balance of fuel from healthy fats, high-fiber carbohydrates, lean proteins, and hydrating fluids
- ☐ Take time to feed myself at regular mealtimes
- ☐ Pay attention to how I feel (mentally and physically) before, during, and after I eat to help me identify which foods help me feel my best
- ☐ Something else: ______________________________

Sacred: How can I use food to connect with the **sacred or spiritual world?**

- ☐ Take five mindful breaths before eating and give thanks for my food. Thank all the people who made it possible for this food to be grown, harvested, and ultimately make its way to my plate. Thank plants and animals for the sacrifice they made with their lives so that I can be fed.
- ☐ Reflect on what "positive" and "negative" energy means to me and make a list of what foods and cooking practices might bring more positive energy into my life.
- ☐ Choose more foods that are as close to their natural state as possible and free of man made chemicals that aren't found in nature.
- ☐ While enjoying a meal, consider how each bite connects me with the energy from the earth including the sunshine, the rainclouds, and all the nutrients from the ground.
- ☐ Something else: ______________________________

Ethical: How can my food choices make the world a **better place for society, animals, or the environment?**

- ☐ Buying locally grown foods directly from a farmer at a farmer's market.
- ☐ Choose foods with no to little plastic packaging to reduce landfill waste.
- ☐ Bringing my reusable shopping bag to the grocery store.
- ☐ Choose a reusable bottle instead of single-use paper, Styrofoam or plastic bottles.
- ☐ Choosing chicken, fish, eggs, or plant protein instead of red meat (beef, pork).
- ☐ Eating more plant protein (beans, lentils, nuts, tofu) and less animal protein (meat, eggs) to help protect the environment and reduce animal and human suffering.
- ☐ Something else: ______________________________

Want to share the Meaning of Food in Life Survey with others? You can find a full copy of the survey in the back of this book.

NOTES

WEEK 2:
Cooking and Eating with All Five Tastes and Senses

Our bodies are designed to enjoy food with all five tastes and all five senses.

The five tastes

The human tongue can detect five different tastes: **sweet**, **sour**, **bitter**, **salty** and **savory** (**umami**). Below are a few example foods or cooking ingredients for each of the five tastes.

Sweet	Salty	Sour	Bitter	Savory
Honey	Sea salt	Vinegar	Broccoli	Mushrooms
Maple syrup	Kosher salt	Lemon	Brussels sprouts	Egg yolk
Bananas	Table salt	Lime	Collard greens	Tree nuts
Blueberries	Pretzels	Tart cherries	Coffee	Peanuts
Sweet potatoes		Green apples	Tea	Garlic
Carrots			Cocoa powder	Soy sauce
Peas				Olives
Cinnamon				Tomato paste
				Sardines
				Parmesan cheese

Do you take cream or sugar with your coffee or tea?

Black coffee and tea are bitter foods, and many people add sugar or cream to these drinks to balance out their taste. This is an example of ***flavor layering***, where ingredients with two or more types of tastes are combined to build flavor.

Flavor layering with two or more kinds of taste

Broccoli *(bitter)* + Garlic and Soy Sauce *(savory)*	= Broccoli Stir Fry
Raisins *(bitter)* + Dark Chocolate *(bitter)*	= Chocolate-covered Raisins
Peanut Butter *(savory)* + Apples *(sweet)*	= Apples with Peanut Butter
Strawberries *(sweet)* + Spinach *(bitter)* + Balsamic Vinegar *(sour)*	= Spinach Salad
Lemon Juice *(sour)* + Garlic *(savory)* + Oil	= Lemon Garlic Vinaigrette or Marinade

Activity: Flavors in My Favorite Food

Think about your favorite meal or snack. *What flavors can you find in this food? Can you think of any new additions or ingredient swaps that could add one more type of flavor (sweet, salty, sour, bitter, or savory) to create something slightly new?*

Favorite Meal or Snack: ______________________________

Flavors ***Ingredients*** *(write below)*

- ☐ *Sweet:* ______________________________
- ☐ *Salty:* ______________________________
- ☐ *Sour:* ______________________________
- ☐ *Bitter:* ______________________________
- ☐ *Savory:* ______________________________

New Ingredients (Flavors) to Try: ______________________________

Want to learn more?

Scan the QR code with your phone or visit https://www.wired.com/video/watch/taste-map

Can you find all 5 tastes in this picture?

Food tastes are personal

Personal tastes begin to develop in the womb before we are born and continue to develop over time based on the kinds of foods we experience. Many things can affect personal food tastes, here are just a few:

- **Genetically** some people are born with more taste buds ("supertasters"), while other people are born with much fewer taste buds than the average person. This genetic difference can play a big role in what foods we like and how we season our foods.
- **Human biology** also affects what kinds of foods we like and don't like. The human brain is hardwired to like foods that are sweet, salty, and savory because foods with these flavors contain essential nutrients that are harder to find in nature. Foods that are bitter or sour helped our ancestors to detect foods that could be poisonous. However, many foods that are sour, like lemons, or bitter, like collard greens, can be quite healthy for us.
- **Childhood foods** that we ate at a very young age often shape our personal food tastes into adulthood.

Enjoying food with all five senses

Food can be enjoyed with all five senses, not just taste! When we use all five senses–sight, touch, sound, smell, and taste–we can make eating a more joyful and relaxing experience, even when eating very simple foods, like a handful of nuts or grapes, or a piece of dark chocolate.

Sight

Touch

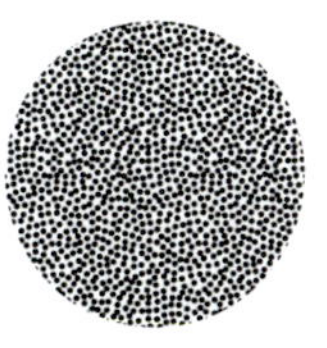
Texture

Smell

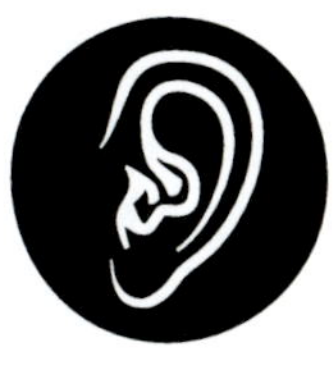
Sound

Taste

While our tongues can only detect five "tastes", our nose can detect more than 10,000 different smells. Together, a food's taste and smell describes its ***flavor***.

Beginning to explore foods with the five senses

How do we begin to enjoy food with all five senses? Consider asking yourself or discussing these questions with others while eating your next meal or snack.

Sight: What color is the food? What shapes do you see? How is it presented on the plate? Even for ordinary foods, is there anything you find beautiful about this food?

Touch and Texture: How does the food feel in your hands or in your mouth? Smooth? Hard? Crumbly? Crunchy? What is the temperature like?

Sound: Did the food make a sound while you cooked it? Does it make a sound when you eat it?

Smell: What does this food smell like? Does it remind you of anything?

Taste: Chew slowly and try to identify ingredients and flavors. How many kinds of flavors (sweet, sour, bitter, salty and savory) can you taste? Does the taste change as it's in your mouth?

> Other qualities of a food, including its temperature, texture, and whether it's eaten raw or cooked will affect its overall taste.

[Continues on the next page...]

Special Note

Both our ability to smell and taste will affect how well we can taste a food. Here are a few things that can affect these two abilities:

Smell: As we age, we gradually lose our sense of smell. People with diabetes and high blood pressure can also lose their sense of smell when these conditions aren't controlled.

Taste: Medications that cause dry mouth can make it harder to taste foods. Drinking heavy amounts of alcohol and smoking tobacco can also affect taste.

As people lose their sense of taste, they may find themselves adding more salt and more sugar than they used to. If you think you have lost some of your sense of taste or smell, here's a few things you can do to help make your meals more enjoyable instead of reaching for the extra salt and sugar:

» Practice enjoying foods with any other senses that are available to you: sight, feeling (texture), or sound.

» Enhance the flavor of foods with acids (vinegar or citrus), spices and herbs.

» Try eating foods at different temperatures to see how eating a food at a warmer or cooler temperature affects its taste. Generally, foods that are eaten very cold or very hot will have less taste than foods that are eaten at a temperature in between.

» Cutting back on tobacco and alcohol can also help to regain losses in taste and smell within just a few weeks.

Try It! Mindful Eating Exercise

Listen to this mindful eating exercise

The following activity can be helpful for anyone looking to deepen their connection with food. *Mindful eating* simply means being present in the moment and using all five senses to connect with your food while eating. Mindful eating can help relax the body during meals and snacks, which prepares the body for digestion. Over time, mindful eating can also provide you with important information about which foods make you feel energetic and happy, and which foods make you feel tired, anxious, or uncomfortable after eating.

Find a simple food item in your home that can be used in the following exercise. Some foods that work well for this exercise include a piece of dark chocolate, a raisin, or a grape. Then follow the steps below to experience mindful eating with this food.

1. **Pick up the food and pretend that you are seeing and sensing this object for the very first time.** What does it look like? What shape is it? What colors? How does it reflect light? Next, maybe investigate more closely how it feels. What is its temperature? Its surface texture? Its density? Perhaps you might also bring it up to your nose. Do you smell anything? Are you salivating? How do you feel about putting this food into your body right now? How does your body feel as you prepare to begin eating at this moment? (Recommended time for this step 3-5 minutes.)

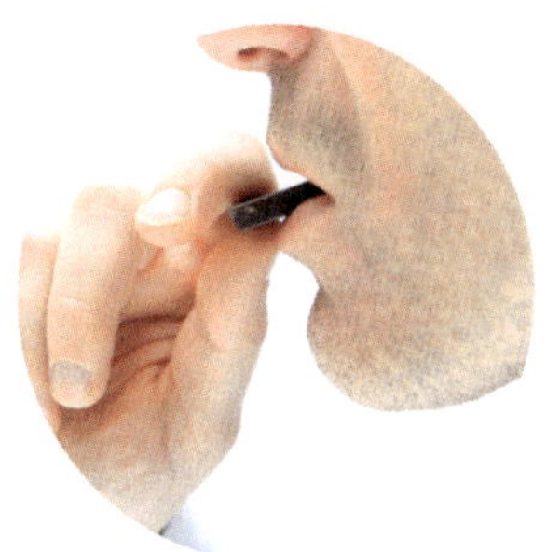

2. **Prepare and begin to receive this food as nourishment in your body.** Be aware of your arm moving to your mouth. How is the food taken into the mouth? Experience the food in your mouth. Chew slowly and focus your full attention on the food's taste and texture. Be aware of any desire you have to rush through this food so that you can have another. Be aware of the intention to swallow before you actually swallow. Notice how far into your body you can still feel the food after you swallow. (Recommended time for this step 2-3 minutes.)

3. **Reflect on what it now feels like to have been nourished by this single piece of food.** (Recommended time for this step 1 minute.)

Benefits of mindful eating

» You may find that your taste buds change and you develop a new appreciation of simple and basic foods.

» You may find that processed and fast foods have less flavor than meals you make with simple ingredients including foods found in nature that are seasoned with spices and herbs.

» You may find yourself feeling satisfied with smaller portions at meals because you notice when you feel full and stop eating.

» You may find yourself feeling less stressed during the day.

» You may find that you crave a big bowl of vegetables sautéed in olive oil and garlic rather than French fries or your other favorite salty snack.

Adapted from The Center for Mind-Body Medicine's Mindful Eating exercise in its Professional Training Program

REFLECTION & TRY IT: EATING MINDFULLY

Reflection: Mindful Eating

What was your experience like eating the food you chose mindfully? Were there particular thoughts, feelings or sensations during this exercise that surprised you?

Try It! Exploring Mindful Eating

- ☐ Try eating a variety of foods mindfully, including your favorite snacks, as well as those foods you don't often eat. Follow the same basic steps as you did the first time.
- ☐ Eat an entire meal mindfully. Write down your observations every time you do this exercise. The more often you eat mindfully, the more you'll learn about your relationship to food.
- ☐ Each time you're about to eat something, notice if you're really hungry. If not, ask yourself: "Why am I eating this food?" Is it out of boredom? Loneliness? Anxiety? Stress? Just notice your answers.

NOTES

WEEK 3:
Food, Mood, Energy, and Stress Resiliency

We are all born with a protective survival instinct known as the stress response.

The body's stress response

Anytime we sense or experience injury, the body's *sympathetic nervous system ("fight or flight")* activates and sends messages to all of the other systems in our body to prepare for a life-threatening event.

While the stress response is very helpful if being chased by a bear or a tiger, our stress response can harm our physical and mental health when it is repeatedly activated by psychological stressors, such as overdue bills. This same stress response also turns on when we worry about things that may happen in the future or repeatedly think about times when our safety was threatened in the past.

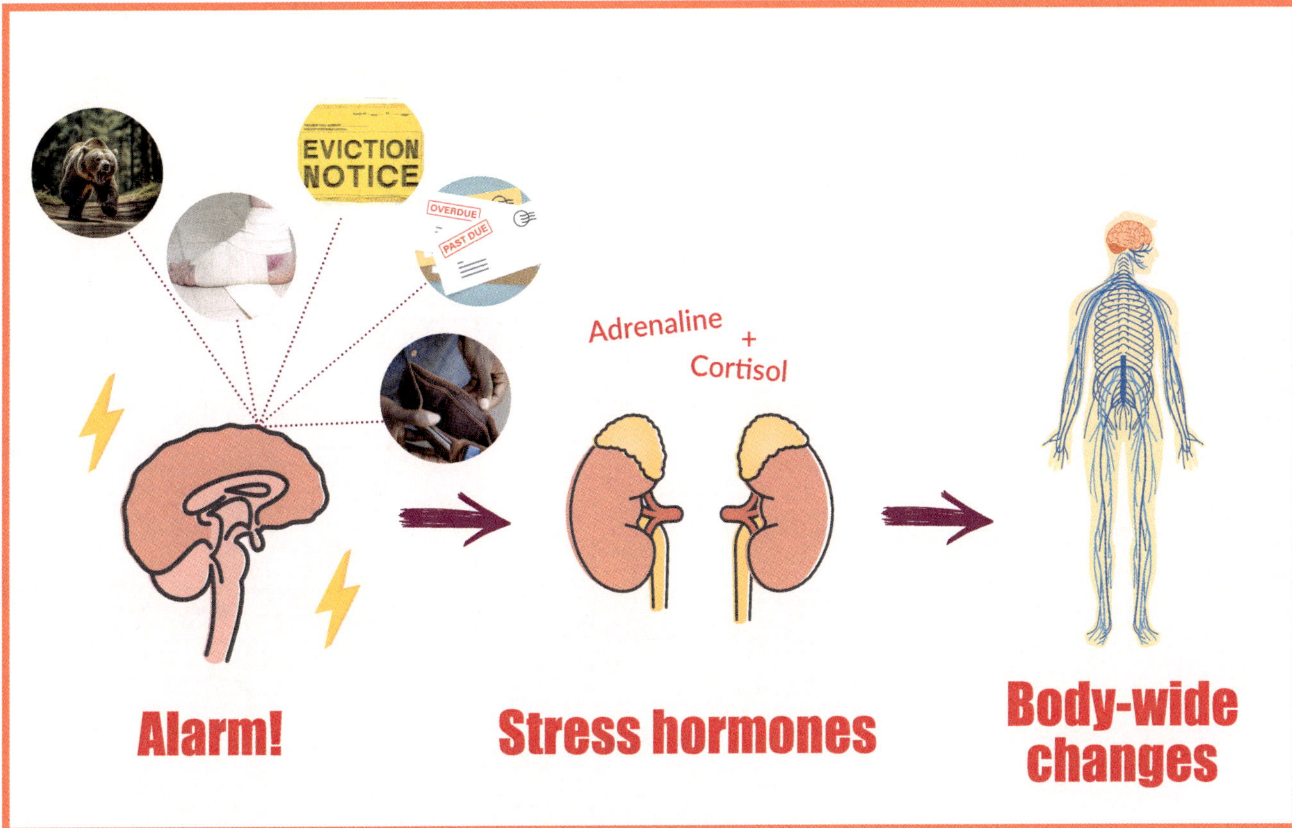

Stress can affect all of the body's systems

When we experience something stressful, the brain tells the kidneys to release stress hormones, like adrenaline and cortisol, that gives our bodies a burst of energy and alertness to better escape from the danger. When this happens, the last thing the brain wants to do is go to sleep! This is why many people have problems sleeping when they are stressed.

Take a few minutes comparing the two pictures on the next pages that show the body in the "fight and flight" (sympathetic) response and in the relaxed "rest and digest" (parasympathetic) state.

How is your body affected at times when you are stressed?

[Continues on the next page...]

STRESS AND YOUR BODY

The human body is built to handle stress... some of the time. Common symptoms of short-term stress include:

The **head** may start to hurt; some people become extra sensitive to light and sound

The **brain** may get distracted with repetitive thoughts, making it difficult to concentrate or sleep

Vision may get blurry, eyelids may twitch, or **eyes** may hurt

Teeth may clench and the mouth may dry out

Skin may get pale, sweaty, or flushed

Muscles may tense or tremble

Breathing may speed up and become shallow; some people hold their breath

Heart rate increases along with blood pressure; this makes it difficult to sleep

Appetite may go up or down; some people experience nausea or even stomach pain

Bowel and bladder control are reduced; some people experience diarrhea or other GI upset.

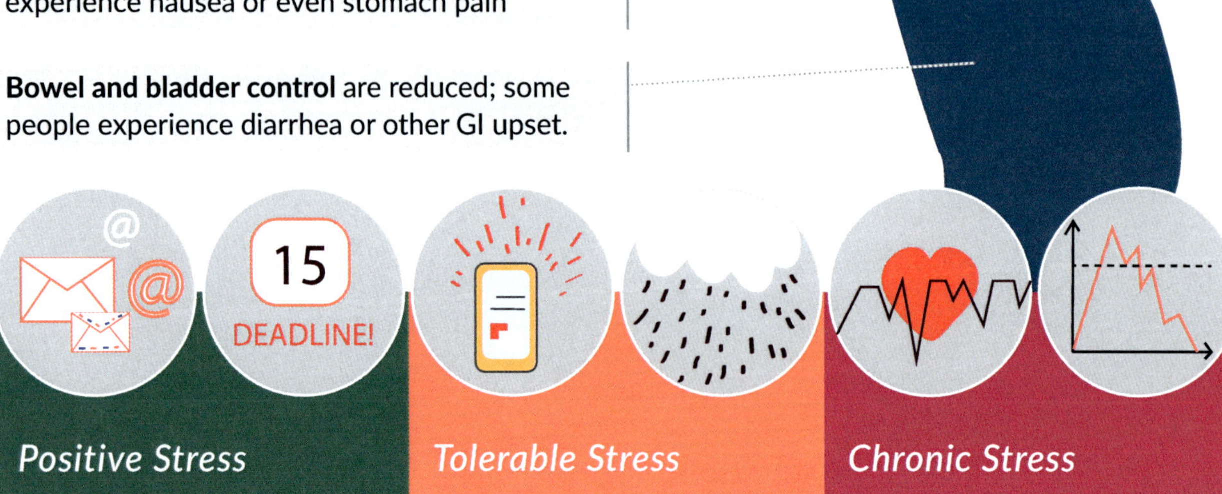

Positive Stress

This stress response isn't always damaging. Positive stress occurs with a change or situation you want, such as starting a new job or moving into a new place. In these situations, a little stress can be motivating.

Tolerable Stress

Tolerable stress occurs when our bodies respond to more serious threats, such as injury or arguments, but return to a calm state easily. Coping skills, loving support, and good health all help the body return to a calm state.

Chronic Stress

When stress is very severe or lasting, however, the body cannot easily return to a calm state. This is chronic stress. Over time, chronic stress can lead to serious health problems.

[Continues on the next page...]

When our body is relaxed, we can better solve problems, feel more connected with others, and heal and repair. Signs of a relaxed state include:

The **brain** is more flexible, focused, creative, curious, and able to make decisions. Ability to fall asleep and stay asleep improves

Pupils constrict improving close-up vision

Mouth produces saliva to support digestion

Muscles and jaw are relaxed

Breathing is even and regular

Heart rate and blood pressure are lowered

The **digestive tract** breaks down food and absorbs nutrients

Bowel and bladder efficiently remove waste from the body

Returning to a relaxed state

Here are some ways you can help your body return to a relaxed state:

Breathing

Inhaling and exhaling slowly through the nose has a calming affect on the mind and body. One simple exercise you can try is to place one hand on your chest and the other on your stomach. While doing so, breathe in slowly through the nose, feeling your stomach expand as the air enters your body. Slowly exhale through your nose, feeling your stomach lower as the air leaves your body. Repeat as many times as desired.

Walking

Walking has a positive affect on overall mood, mental alertness, and energy. The walks do not have to be long. Research shows that a few ten-minute walks scattered throughout the day is enough to see results!

Nature

Being outside in nature can improve your mood and promote a relaxed state of mind. Take a little time throughout the day to simply walk outside and observe the trees, birds, sky, flowers, and other living things. Take a few deep breaths. Reflect on how it makes you feel.

Activity: My Body Stressed and Relaxed

Draw yourself under stress and then draw yourself feeling safe and relaxed. Add labels to tell what you are thinking and feeling in each picture.

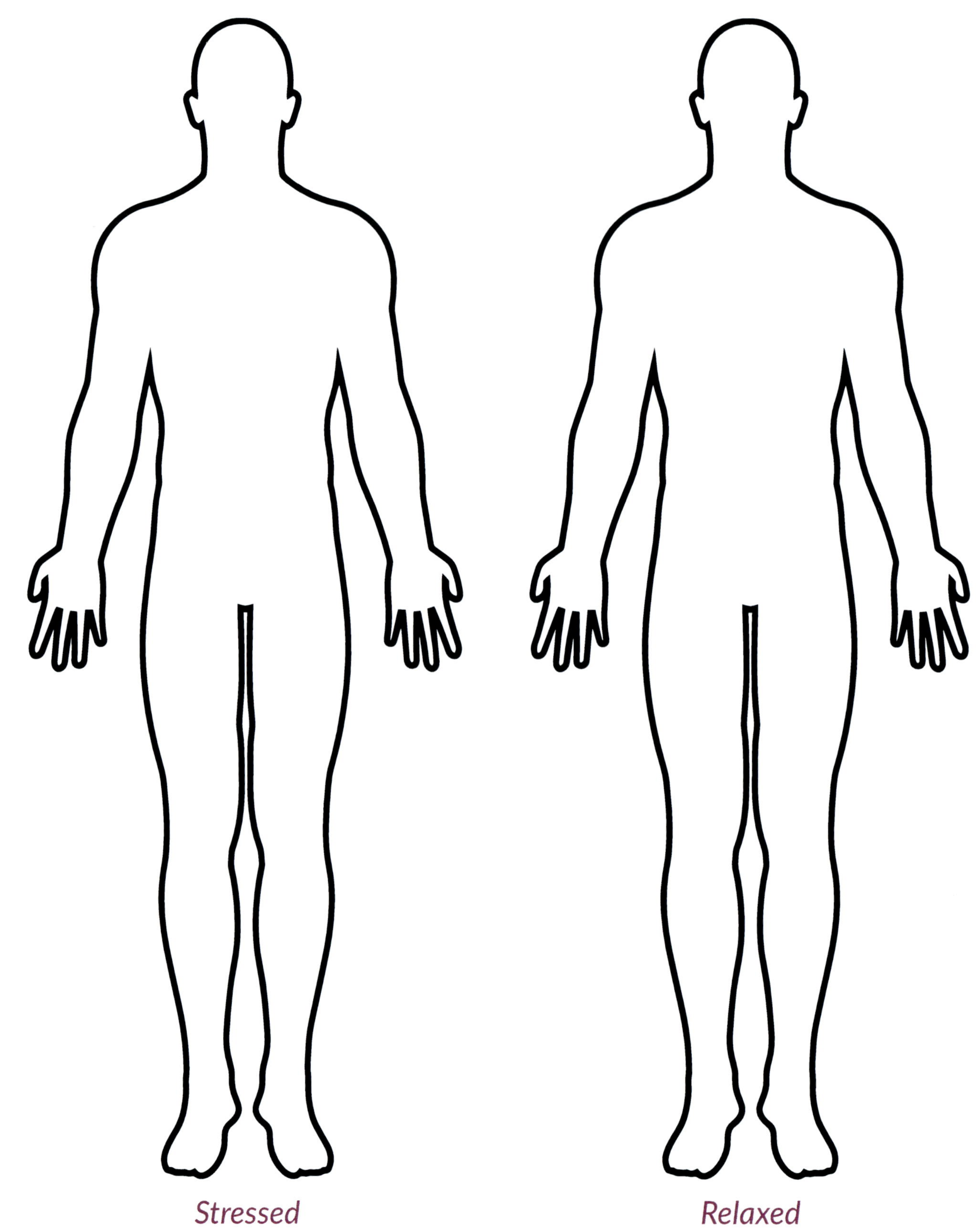

Stress is a normal part of life, but our bodies need time to recover in between each stress response.

Since the stress response begins with what we perceive in our brains, it is most often triggered by things we are worrying about or remembering from our past rather than immediate physical dangers. **When we find ourselves worrying or repeatedly thinking about negative past experiences, we can practice mindfulness to help bring our focus to the present moment instead.** There are several mindfulness activities located in the back of the book if you'd like to give any of these a try.

How is food related to stress?

Food can also have a positive or a negative impact on how well our bodies react to and recover from stressors. Food can also shape our moods. For people in recovery, balanced nutrition can also help us withstand cravings and manage stressful events that may trigger a relapse.

Can You Relate?

"Stress–both past and present–affects my eating habits."

Many people crave **sugar**, **caffeine**, or **highly processed snacks** when stressed, tired, or "down." These provide quick energy or pleasure. But they can also cause a crash when the energy wears off, ultimately making energy or mood even worse. Some people may skip meals when they are anxious, tired, or in a hurry. Skipping meals can also cause mood or energy crashes and lead to overeating food later.

Our bodies need **lean proteins**, **healthy fats**, **fiber-rich carbohydrates**, and **hydrating fluids** for proper fueling. When these fuel sources are imbalanced, our mental and physical health can suffer. Choosing a fuel source from each of these four areas can support a healthy mood, immune system, and stable blood sugar.

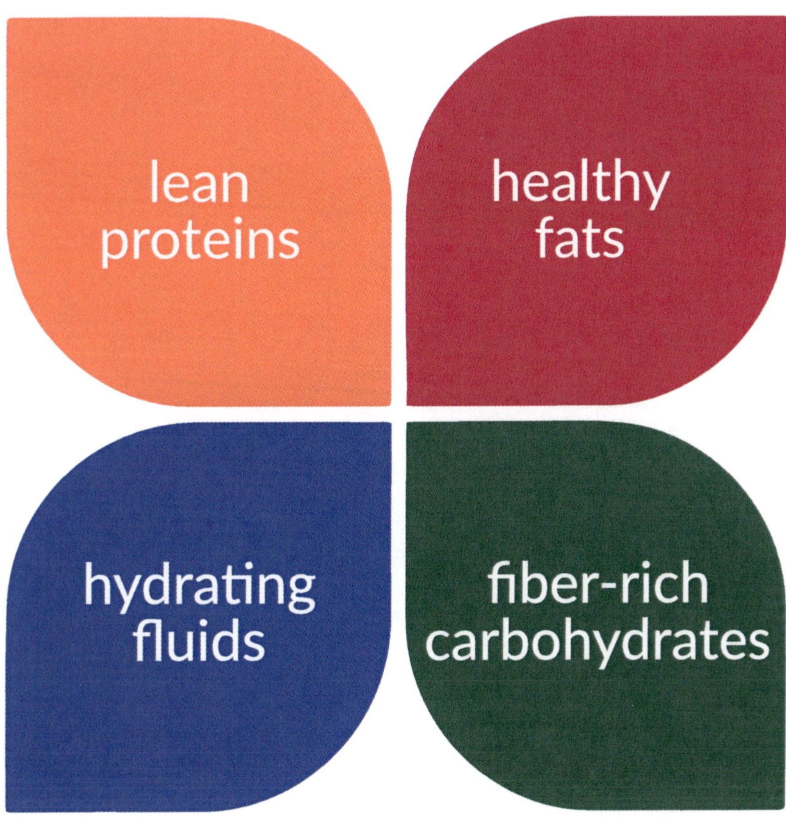

My fuel sources

Below is a list of example foods that provide proteins, healthy fats, high fiber carbohydrates, and hydrating fluids. Check the box for each food that you enjoy eating or would be willing to eat more often to help balance out each of your meals. Try rounding your meal out with a few nutrient boosters and herbs and spices to help support your body even more.

lean proteins | healthy fats | hydrating fluids | fiber-rich carbohydrates

● also supplies healthy fats ● also supplies high-fiber carbohydrates
● also supplies healthy proteins

Step 1

Proteins

- ☐ Salmon ●
- ☐ Tuna ●
- ☐ Sardines ●
- ☐ Tofu ●

- ☐ Lentils ●
- ☐ Lentil or chickpea pasta ●
- ☐ Beans ●

- ☐ Skinless chicken
- ☐ Extra-lean beef
- ☐ Eggs
- ☐ Cottage cheese

- ☐ Others: ______

High-Fiber Carbohydrates

- ☐ Fresh, frozen, freeze-dried fruits
- ☐ Sweet potatoes
- ☐ Oats
- ☐ Barley
- ☐ 100% Whole grain bread
- ☐ 100% Whole grain cereals
- ☐ Corn
- ☐ Popcorn
- ☐ Bulgur wheat
- ☐ Quinoa
- ☐ Others: ______

Hydrating Fluids

- ☐ Water
- ☐ Sparkling water
- ☐ Black tea
- ☐ Green tea
- ☐ Herbal tea (caffeine free)

Healthy Fats

- ☐ Almonds ●
- ☐ Cashews ●
- ☐ Peanuts ●
- ☐ Sunflower seeds ●
- ☐ Walnuts ●
- ☐ Natural peanut butter, sunbutter, nut butter ●
- ☐ Olives
- ☐ Olive, canola, or avocado oil
- ☐ Flaxseed
- ☐ Almond and cashew milk
- ☐ Others: ______

Step 2

Nutrient Boosters

- ☐ Non-starchy fresh, frozen, or freeze-dried vegetables, such as red bell peppers, onions, spinach, or carrots
- ☐ Low-sodium vegetable juice

Anti-inflammatory spices and herbs

- ☐ Turmeric
- ☐ Curry powder
- ☐ Chili powder
- ☐ Crushed red pepper
- ☐ Italian seasoning, garlic, ginger

Can You Relate?

"If you eat well, it helps you cope and deal with stress better."

How big is a serving?

Everybody's nutrition needs are unique. Finding the portion size that's right for you is an important part of balanced meals.

When we eat too much or too little, our energy levels can suffer. You can use the serving size examples below as a starting place for standard portions. You may need to adjust your portion sizes for certain foods to find the right balance for you.

Do you usually eat more than these portions, or less?

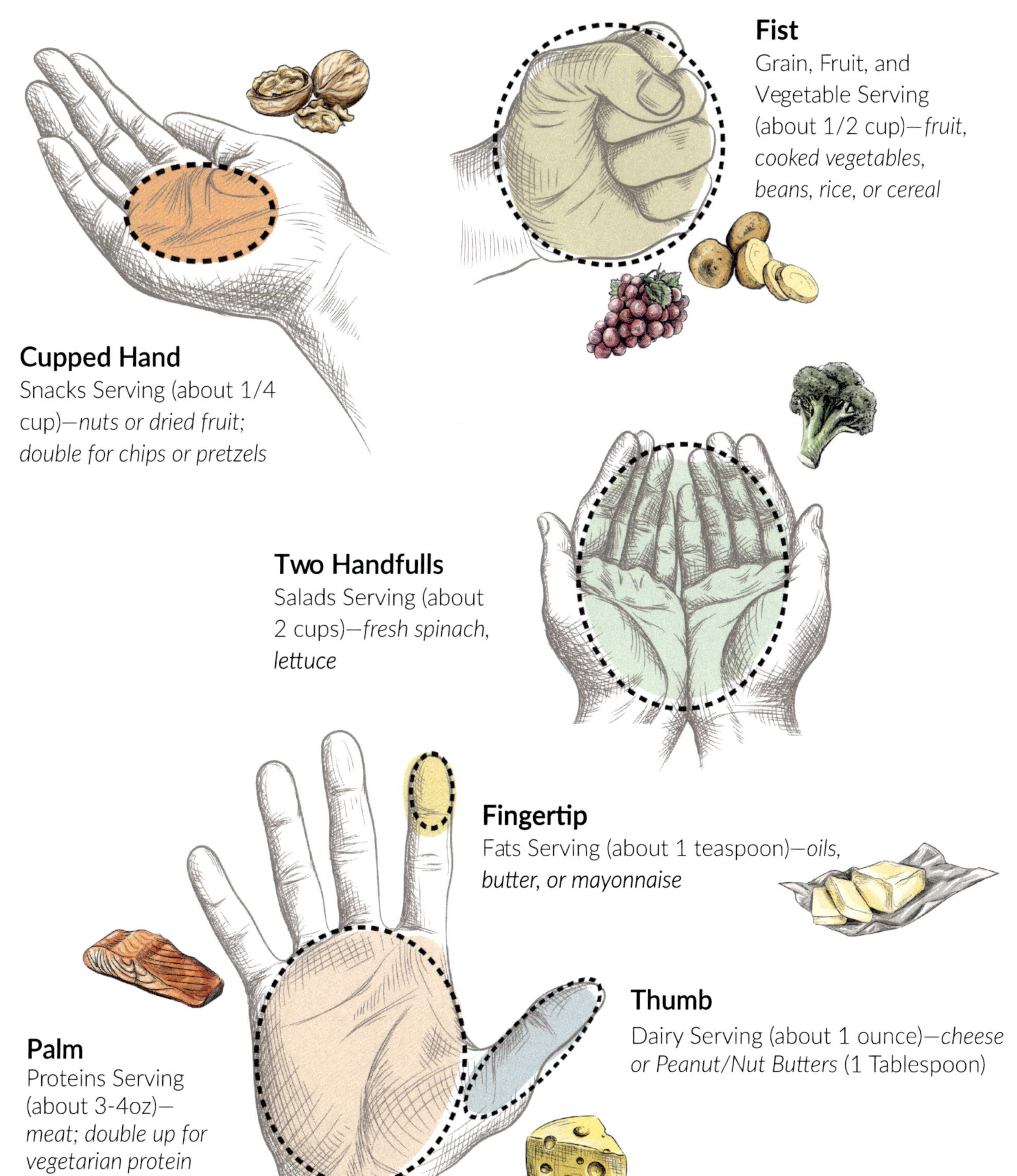

Fist
Grain, Fruit, and Vegetable Serving (about 1/2 cup)—*fruit, cooked vegetables, beans, rice, or cereal*

Cupped Hand
Snacks Serving (about 1/4 cup)—*nuts or dried fruit; double for chips or pretzels*

Two Handfulls
Salads Serving (about 2 cups)—*fresh spinach, lettuce*

Fingertip
Fats Serving (about 1 teaspoon)—*oils, butter, or mayonnaise*

Thumb
Dairy Serving (about 1 ounce)—*cheese or Peanut/Nut Butters* (1 Tablespoon)

Palm
Proteins Serving (about 3-4oz)—*meat; double up for vegetarian protein*

REFLECTION: STRESS AND EATING

Reflection: Stress, Food, and Eating

People eat for many different reasons. Though most animals eat when they're hungry and stop when they're full, human beings often eat to fulfill emotional needs and don't stop when their physical hunger is satisfied. Or, their emotions may be overwhelming, and they may forget to eat. For this week's reflection, think about the following:

Can You Relate?

"I'm an emotional eater, so I know that I eat when I'm upset. I eat for comfort, I eat for boredom, I eat when I'm hungry, when I'm not hungry. So, food is a comfort for me, food is there to be comforting when everything else is overwhelming, in particular sweets."

1. ***How does stress affect my relationship with food? How does stress affect my hunger? How does stress affect my satiety (feeling satisfied after eating)?***

2. ***What are some positive ways that I can use food or meal times to help myself and those I care about deal with chronic stress? What about some non-food ways?***

[Continues on the next page...]

Try It! Food and Energy Experiments

Each of us is biochemically unique and there is no single diet that is right for everyone.

Over the next week, consider trying one or more of the following experiments to see whether they improve your mood or energy. Through mindful eating and a few personal experiments, we can discover which foods give us energy and which foods may be causing us problems. Some people may notice a difference within days and for others it may take several weeks.

- ☐ If you don't regularly drink water, drink 4-8 cups (32-64 ounces) of plain water each day. If you don't like the taste of plain water, try adding a few slices of cut fruit to a pitcher the night before. Drinking water regularly can give you an awareness of when you are dehydrated, which is a cause of low energy for some people.
- ☐ If you are used to eating donuts, muffins, or other sweet foods for breakfast, try starting your day with some protein to help balance out the carbohydrates and fats. This could be a hard-boiled egg, omelet, or even some scrambled tofu. You might consider swapping out the sweet grain for a 100% whole grain cereal or oatmeal topped with cinnamon. This may help you to notice how a high-sugar breakfast may be affecting your energy levels.
- ☐ Replace soda with iced tea that is naturally sweetened with sliced oranges or lemons (no other added sugar). Fruity herbal teas like hibiscus work great for this. Notice if the tea can help to naturally boost your energy without the crash and burn effects of the added sugars that come from soda.
- ☐ If you usually eat only one meal per day, consider nourishing your body at least one more time each day. Simple options might be: a handful of nuts or peanut butter with a piece of fruit; a small bowl of oatmeal topped with walnuts; or a small foil pack of chicken or salmon with a few crackers.
- ☐ Something else: ______________________________

Your body deserves (and needs) a relaxed eating experience.

Another way for nourishing our resilience to stress is creating protected time in our day that is just for eating. This allows your body to focus on the food that you are eating and the digestion process. Below are several examples of how to create a more relaxed eating experience at home.

- ☐ Practice mindful eating exercise with the first bite of each meal.
- ☐ Take a moment to reflect upon who might have grown or created this meal for you. In your mind, thank them for helping you to nourish your body.
- ☐ Turn off the TV and your cell phone while eating. Turn on some relaxing music, if you'd like.
- ☐ Something else: ______________________________

NOTES

WEEK 4:
Resiliency in the Kitchen

The body has the capacity to adapt and recover from challenges. This is known as resilience.

Making your kitchen work for you

The kitchen is considered the heart of the home in many cultures, but sometimes fatigue, chronic pain, or busy schedules can keep us from using this space to better nourish ourselves with good food. ***Mise en place*** is a French cooking term that means "everything in its place". This practice can help set us up for success by helping to make cooking more time and energy efficient. There are many free changes we can make to our kitchen space to help accomplish this. Here are a few suggestions to help get you started:

Kitchen Space	Energy and Time Saving Tips
Food Storage  	» Organize healthy food staples so that shelf-stable lean proteins, whole grains, healthy fats, and other essential cooking staples are each grouped together, easy to see and within reach. » Showcase foods in the front and center of your refrigerator, pantry, and countertop that you want to eat more often. » Keep a few bags of vegetables in the freezer—no need to wash or chop! » Keep a few quick, no cook options on hand for days when you don't feel like cooking.
Non-Food Storage 	» Store everyday dishes and silverware close to the sink or dishwasher. » Store pots, pans, and other cooking utensils near the stove or oven. » Store re-usable dish cloths in an easy to reach place for anytime you need to clean up a mess or need a pot holder.
Prep Space 	» Put away any unused or rarely used appliances or tools to clear your counter space. » Move knives, cutting boards, spices, and other utensils as close as possible to the area where you will prepare food. » Use a bowl or trash can at the end of the counter to toss things like pits, peels, and cores as you cook.
Cooking 	» Place cooking utensils in a crock near the stove so they are easy to reach. » If you have difficulty standing, use a stool or chair while you cook. » Try different cooking tools that best fit your needs. Slow cookers (crock-pots) and rice cookers are great time savers and can be found at second-hand stores.

How to read a recipe

If you are new to cooking, basic recipes can be a great place to help you get started.

Basic Vinaigrette

Prep Time: 5 min **Cook Time:** 0 min **Yield**: 8 servings

Ingredients:

- ¾ cup olive oil
- ¼ cup lemon juice or apple cider vinegar
- 2-3 tablespoons water
- ½ teaspoon salt
- ¼ teaspoon black pepper

Directions:

1. Whisk all ingredients in a bowl with a fork or shake everything together in a lidded jar.
2. Use immediately or store in refrigerator for up to 1 week.

1. Read the recipe all the way through before starting.
   - Make sure you have all the items you need and enough time for the recipe.
   - Look up any words you don't know.
   - When an ingredient is optional or if desired, you don't have to use it unless you want to.
   - If necessary, preheat the oven while you prepare.
2. Prepare ingredients for the recipe before you start to cook.
   - If a recipe calls for chopped onion, for example, do the chopping now.
3. Measure carefully.
   - It helps to know abbreviations: **c.** = cup, **T.** or **tbsp**. = tablespoon, **t.** or **tsp**. = teaspoon. It's also helpful to know measurement shortcuts. For example:
     - 4 tablespoons = ¼ cup
     - 3 teaspoons = 1 tablespoon
4. Pay attention to the order of the steps.
5. If you change your recipe as you cook, make a note. That way you can prepare the dish exactly the same way next time—or not!

What tricks do you know for cooking for one?

It's possible to eat well-balanced meals at home without a lot of effort, even if you live alone. Here are a few ideas for saving time and energy:

» **Plan your meals each week.** Use the same ingredients in many meals but in different ways. For example, buy vegetables that can be eaten both cooked and raw like celery; use in soups, sandwiches, stir-fries and salads.

» **Cook or prep when you have the most energy.** Cut up fruits and vegetables to store, or prep an entire meal. Dinner doesn't have to be the biggest meal of the day. If you have more energy and time in the middle of the day, eat your biggest meal then.

» **Keep a stocked pantry.** You'll be more likely to cook if you already have long lasting ingredients like dried and canned vegetables, dried and canned fruit, canned beans, quick-cooking whole grains, and seasonings.

» **Eat the most perishable produce first** like lettuce, and save heartier produce like broccoli. Even better—stock up on vegetables like winter squash, onions, and potatoes that last for months outside the fridge. Dried vegetables are another great option to keep on hand - use just what you need and save the rest for later!

» **Cook larger batches and freeze.** Cook batches of grains and beans and freeze for easy additions to meals. Soups and casseroles freeze well in smaller portions.

» **Bring extras to a friend or neighbor, or invite them over to share a meal.** Hopefully, they will return the favor!

Sample meals

» Eggs are a great single-serving dish. Add veggies, cheese and whole grain toast to make a satisfying meal.

» Start with a dried grain like rice or pasta, add veggies (fresh, frozen or canned), a protein like salmon (fresh, frozen, or canned), and a sauce or flavorings like olive oil and garlic, or soy sauce and ginger.

» Use cooked chicken in a salad with nuts and fruit or on a sandwich with whole wheat bread.

» Make an Asian inspired noodle dish: mix cooked pasta or soak rice noodles with stir-fried veggies and a mixture of soy sauce and peanut butter.

» Mix cooked couscous or quinoa with a dressing of vinegar, olive oil, salt and pepper and lots of fresh veggies, black beans and canned corn.

Reflection: Your Favorite Meal

Is there a source of healthy proteins, high-fiber carbohydrates, healthy fats in your favorite meal for one? If not, what ingredient(s) could you add or replace?

___

___

___

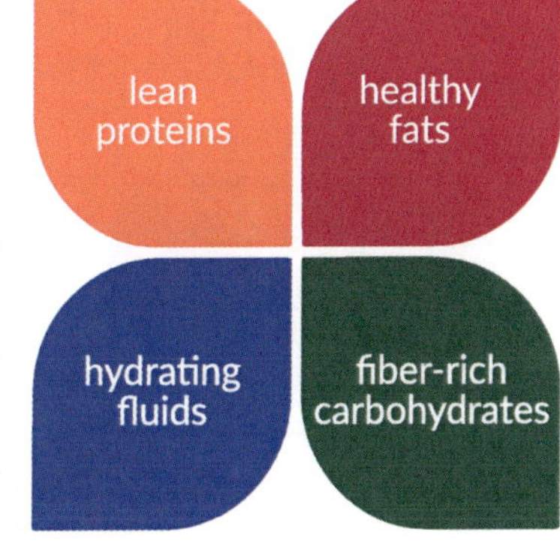
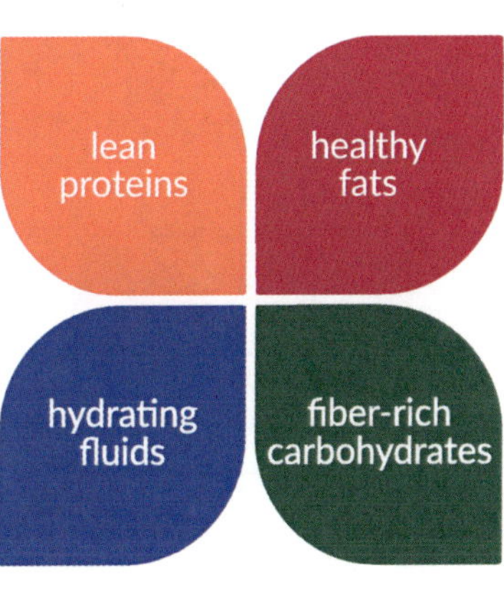

MINDFUL MEAL PLANNING

Activity: Mindful Meal Planning

Draw or describe a nourishing meal for you or you and your family. Consider not only the experience of eating the meal, but the shopping and planning required, and any routines or rituals you enjoy.

Don't go into detail – just visualize some images, or write a few descriptive adjectives. For example, I would describe a nourishing but low-stress meal to be quick preparation, fresh ingredients, my whole family in attendance.

Think about what you may already have, then make a list of what you'll need.

1. ______________________
2. ______________________
3. ______________________
4. ______________________
5. ______________________
6. ______________________
7. ______________________
8. ______________________
9. ______________________
10. ______________________
11. ______________________
12. ______________________

Activity: Making a Kitchen Anchor

Whether you struggle to enjoy cooking or love it, creating a meaningful space in your kitchen can help set a positive mood from the moment you step in the room. Seeing your meaningful space, or ***kitchen anchor***, can spark a smile or fill your heart with positive feelings, good memories, or a sense of peace. It can be a visual reminder of your intentions, people who inspire you, things you are grateful for, or the values that center your life.

Here are a few simple steps to set up your meaningful space or kitchen anchor:

1. **Pick a place!** Ideally it will be somewhere you can see immediately when entering your kitchen. It could be a windowsill, on a shelf, on a counter, or a table.

2. **Choose the items you want to decorate your space**. This could be anything small that is meaningful to you. For example,
   - Add items that remind you of nature and your impact on the environment around you. These could be acorns or a fallen leaf that caught your eye in the fall, a flower that bloomed in your yard, seeds, or even a live plant.
   - Add items that make you think of people you love or who inspire you. In addition to photos, this could be trinkets that bring cherished memories, like a ticket stub or special rock.
   - Add items that connect to you spiritually, whether that is an object like a candle or words like a poem, prayer, or mantra.
   - Add items that represent your intentions, goals for yourself, or remind you to take care of yourself. These could include a piece of fruit, a pen, or a message you have written to yourself and folded up.

3. As you place your items and decorate your space, **focus on the items and the feelings it brings you like peace, comfort, or happiness.**

4. **Take a step back and check that your space is visually appealing to you.** Try to have a variety of colors and textures. Can you add any smells or sounds to your space?

5. **Don't clutter your anchor with too many things.** Be choosy and intentional about the items you place. Spend a little time reflecting on your meaningful space each day. Rotate items out seasonally or whenever you would like. The act of refreshing the space can be a practice in appreciation itself. The possibilities are endless!

*Share a picture of your kitchen anchor at **HowDoYouNourish.org***

REFLECTION & TRY IT: MEANINGFUL KITCHENS

Try It! Bring some mise en place to your kitchen.

Using the table on page 49 of this week's module, look for small changes you can make in your kitchen so that cooking can be more enjoyable and easy to do. Now, make these changes and cook a meal.

Reflection

What differences did you notice in your cooking experience? What additional changes can you plan to make in the future?

Try It! Make a kitchen anchor

Now, plan and create an anchor on your own or create one together with others in your home. Look back at your Meaning of Food in My Life survey results from Week 1 and the meanings that you wanted to develop or explore more.

Reflection

How might a kitchen anchor remind or encourage you to connect with those meanings when you eat each day? Where might an anchor fit best in your kitchen?

Try It! Use a dedicated space for eating

The place where we eat our food can be a reminder to focus on the here-and-now of eating. This might be a dining table, on the floor, on a stool at the counter, or any other dedicated space to eating. If this area is easily cluttered, take time to keep it clean this week and enjoy a meal in this area at least once.

Reflection

How was your experience of eating this meal different from eating a meal in the car, on the phone, or in front of the TV?

MONTH 2: MY PERSONAL FOOD STORY

In this section, you are invited to explore:

- Learn how to use herbs and spices to transform the flavor of everyday foods
- Discover how I can support a healthy mind through nourishing meals that support a healthy gut
- Add color to my meals in creative and easy ways using different kinds of fruits and vegetables
- Find new ways to create filling, satisfying meals with lean proteins and healthy fats

WEEK 5:
Building Flavors with Spices And Herbs

Want to discover new flavors in everyday foods? Start with a little spice

Fast food companies mostly rely on two ingredients–sugar and salt–to cheaply season foods. While sugar and salt can reliably enhance the flavor of just about any food, they can also place limits on how deeply we experience that food. Our tongues can only detect five "tastes", but our nose can detect more than 10,000 different smells. **Because of their powerful smell and taste, spices and herbs can quickly transform the overall flavor of our everyday foods.** When we use spices or herbs to season our meals, we can create an endless variety of sensory experiences and flavors that sugar and salt can't beat.

 *Activity: Spices in Everyday Foods*

Many of our favorite homemade meals have at least one herb or spice within them that are essential to the making of that food. Match these foods to their "magic" (spice or herb) ingredients:

Food	***Ingredients***
 oatmeal cookies	 coriander, turmeric, cumin, black pepper, chili powder, ginger
 lasagna	 chili powder, cumin
 chicken noodle soup	 cinnamon, nutmeg
 beef tacos	 rosemary, sage
 curry dishes	 basil, oregano

Answer key:
Oatmeal cookies: cinnamon, nutmeg; Lasagna: basil, oregano; Chicken noodle soup: rosemary, sage; Beef tacos: chili powder, cumin; Curry dishes: coriander, turmeric, cumin, black pepper, chili powder, ginger

FLAVORS AROUND THE GLOBE

Unlike salt and sugar, herbs and spices can also help improve our health! These special ingredients are packed with antioxidants that protect our cells from damage. We only need about **1 teaspoon per day** of dried herbs or spices to reap their benefits. Here are a few examples of dried herbs and spices commonly used in different traditional cuisines around the globe.

Mexican

- cumin
- oregano
- chili powder
- garlic powder

Eastern

- cumin
- chili powder
- ginger
- garlic powder
- cinnamon

Indian

- cumin
- chili powder
- ginger
- garlic powder
- curry powder

Italian

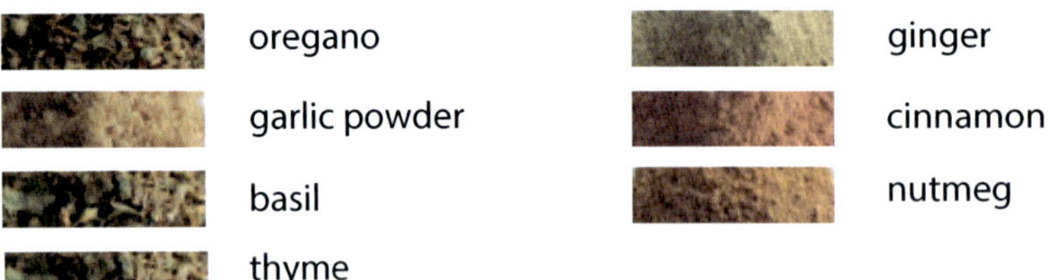

- oregano
- garlic powder
- basil
- thyme

Dessert

- ginger
- cinnamon
- nutmeg

Activity: Exploring the Spice Wheel

A spice wheel can help us explore the different flavor profiles of spices and herbs. It can help us better understand the flavors behind those seasonings that we like, and invite us to explore what kinds of spices or herbs you might like to try.

Take a few moments exploring your spice wheel. Then, consider answering the following questions:

1. There are 2 types of cinnamon on the wheel, and they aren't next to each other. Find sweet cinnamon and Cassia cinnamon on the wheel. Both of these cinnamons were provided in your NOURISH box. Take each of these cinnamons out and do a side by side smell test and taste test. ***What differences do you notice in how these two spices taste and smell?***

2. We don't generally eat pine trees, but there are a few 'piney' and 'resinous' flavors on the wheel. Find these dried herbs on the "Herbal Warm" section of the spice wheel. A few of these example herbs were included in your NOURISH box. What are they? Consider smelling each one. ***What memories or other associations do these bring up?***

Special Note

Scientists aren't sure exactly why, but when we cook with spices and herbs, their smells may unlock memories or stir up emotions. If you become upset during any of these activities, you can take a break and practice any of the relaxation exercises in the back of this book.

3. In this month's NOURISH box, there is a small bag of fennel seeds. Take a seed or two out of the bag, pop it in your mouth and plug your nose. Chew for a couple seconds then release your plugged nose. ***What's different? Do you picture any colors when you unplug your nose?***

4. Find a familiar spice on the wheel and then see if there are any in that section that you've never cooked with. Then, experiment with a new spice that is the same section as the familiar spice. See how the new flavor creates a different, yet familiar taste experience. ***What was your experience like?***

Thank you to Curio Spices for allowing use of their Spice Wheel and developing these exercises.

Reflection: Exploring Our Food Histories

Think about the following questions and use the space below to record your ideas. You can also use these questions to discuss with friends, family, or a roommate.

1. ***Is there a particular food or meal you associate with a happy memory? Describe the memory and the foods. How does it make you feel to write about this happy time in your life?***

2. ***How do you know when food is made or offered with love? What spices, herbs, or other smells do you associate with love?***

3. ***What health issues run in your family? Are any of these problems negatively affected by eating high amounts of sugar or salt, such as type 2 diabetes, depression, or high blood pressure? How might spices and herbs (along with less sugar and salt) help to reduce your risk for these conditions?***

NOTES

WEEK 6:
Our Body's Second Brain

"Health does not always come from medicine. Most of the time, it comes from peace of mind, peace of heart, peace of soul. It comes from laughter and love" - Unknown

Our digestive system (the "gut") plays a huge role in our overall well-being

Without our digestive system, we could not break down food to get energy and all the other nutrients that our body needs. But, that's not all our gut does for us!

Here are the major ways that our gut impacts our mental and physical well-being beyond just breaking down food:

- » Our gut sends and receives messages to and from the brain through the ***gut-brain axis***
- » Our gut creates ***serotonin*** (the "happy" hormone), which affects our mood, sleep, regularity, and bone health
- » Our gut is connected to the ***vagus nerve***, which is used to slow the stress response and stimulate relaxation
- » Our gut is the home to trillions of tiny microbial cells (***"microbiome"***) that play a big role in immunity, chronic inflammation, and possibly chronic pain.

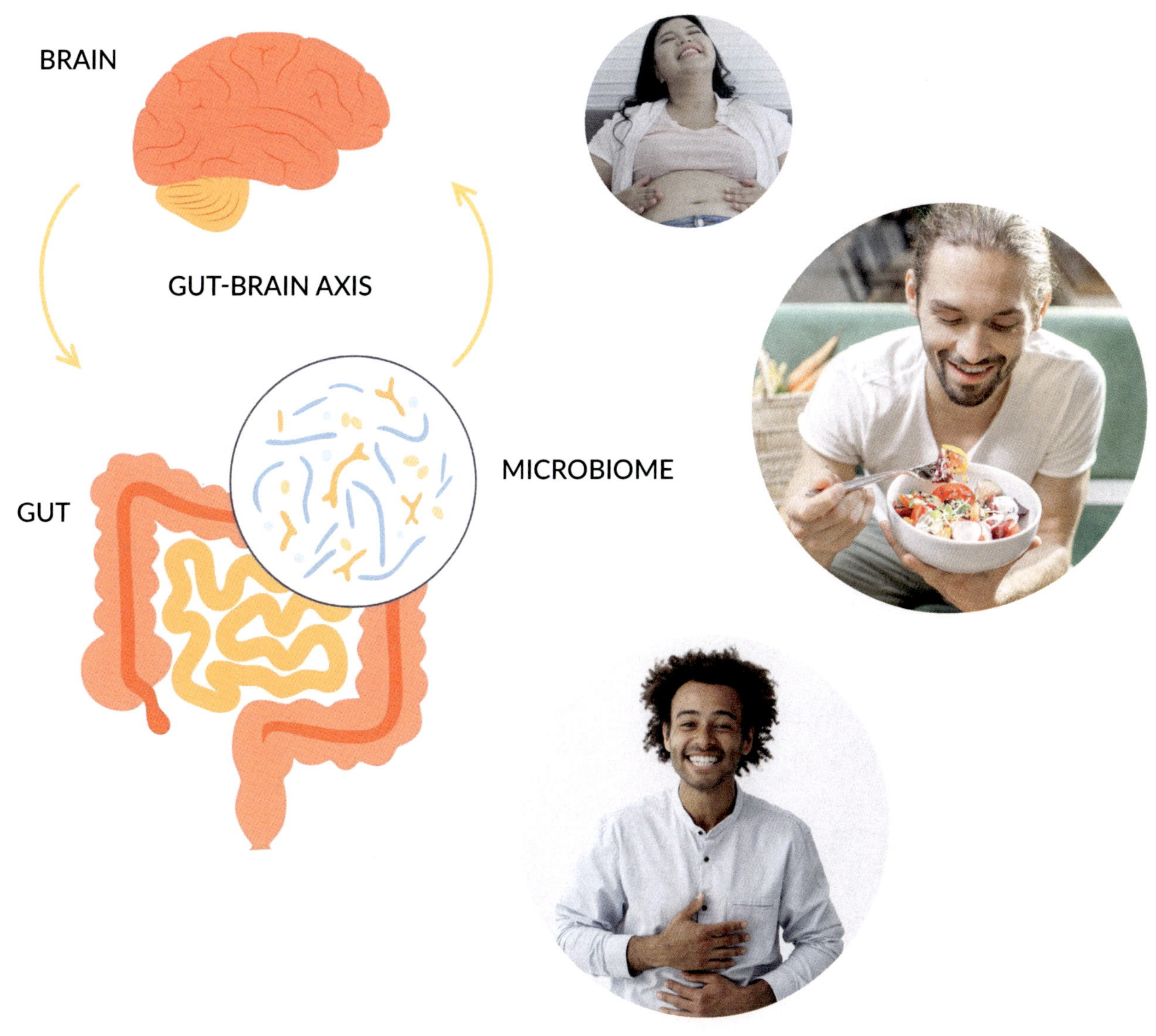

CARING FOR OUR DIGESTIVE SYSTEM

Caring for our digestive system can help us harness its power for healing.

Gut-brain axis

The ***gut-brain axis*** is a two-way pathway where the gut and brain talk with each other and work together. A healthy gut-brain axis supports greater feelings of happiness, good sleep, and regularity while an unhealthy gut-brain axis is linked to depression, anxiety, or digestive issues. **We can support a healthy gut-brain axis by activating our vagus nerve and taking time to feed our gut's microbiome.**

Gut-Brain Axis

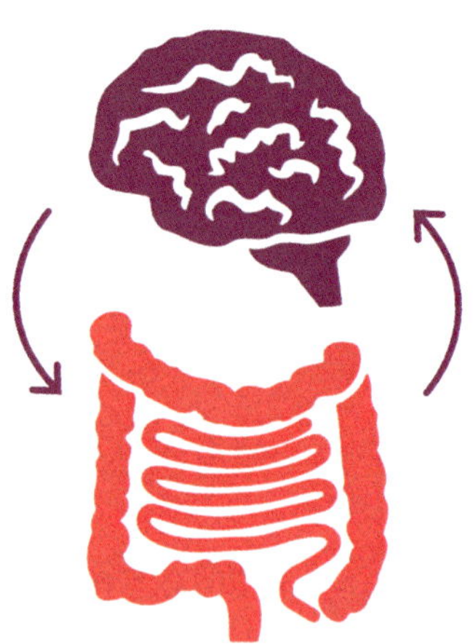

Activating our vagus nerve

The vagus nerve got its name from the Latin word for "wandering." This large nerve has connections from our brain stem all the way through our digestive system down to our colon (large intestine). It is connected to each of the vital organs that are part of our digestive system, including the liver, gallbladder, and kidneys. When we stimulate our vagus nerve, we are supporting the healthy functioning of all these parts of our body.

Have you ever felt "butterflies in your stomach" when you were nervous? Or have you felt "sick to your stomach" when you felt threatened or lost something important to you? When we experience stress (read more in Week 3), the body's digestive system slows down or stops working normally. This is why some people experience diarrhea, loss of appetite, or upset stomach when they feel stressed. We can put the "brake" on the stress response by doing things that stimulate the vagus nerve.

Vagus Nerve
parasympathetic nervous system

LUNGS
HEART
LIVER
STOMACH
INTESTINES

Here are a few options you can try to "talk to" or "wake up" your vagus nerve:

- Slow, deep breathing
- Laughing, singing, humming
- Yoga or tai chi
- Cold showers

Another way to support a healthy gut is through feeding its ***microbiome***. The microbiome is made up of trillions of tiny microbial cells that live on and in our bodies. Most of these microbial cells live in our gut and play a big role in health and disease.

A healthy microbiome can stabilize mood, increase energy, prevent sickness, and support healthy digestion. An unbalanced microbiome can lead to depression, inflammatory bowel disease, obesity, and more. Just like a garden, there are things we can do to nourish our microbiome to help keep it balanced so that it can keep taking care of us.

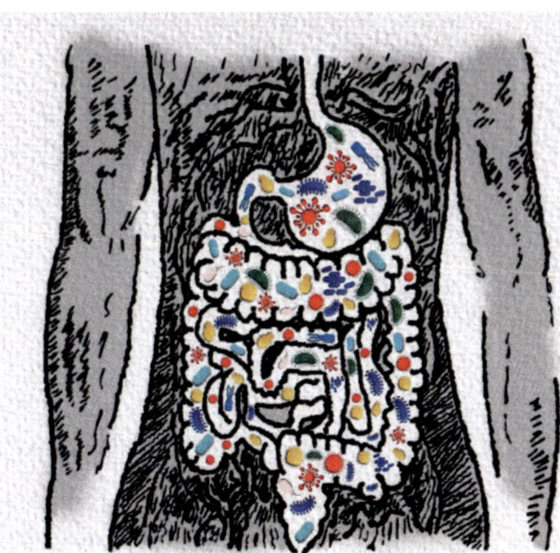

Here are a few things you can do to feed your gut's microbiome to keep it healthy and strong:

Feed it what it needs.

The microbiome gets its nutrition from fiber (***prebiotics***). Eating high-fiber foods, including whole grains, fruit, vegetables, nuts, seeds, lentils, and beans, give the "good" bacteria what it needs to survive. Most people only eat about ⅓ of the fiber that is needed to keep their microbiome well-fed.

Enjoy cultured and fermented foods.

Yogurt, sauerkraut, kimchi, and tempeh all contain healthy ***probiotic*** cultures that support a healthy microbiome.

Limit or avoid alcohol.

Alcohol can harm the friendly bacteria in our guts, while feeding the growth of other bacteria that are linked to chronic inflammation, pain, and cancer.

WHAT ARE WHOLE GRAINS?

Whole grains: A key fuel source for a healthy gut, mind, and body

Fiber is the essential fuel source for the gut microbiome, and whole grains are a great option for meeting these fiber needs. A whole grain kernel is an edible seed that supplies everything needed to make a new plant. When we eat whole grains, these nutrients become a great source of nutrition to help fuel our bodies and feed our microbiome.

Nature's perfect package

Each part of the whole grain provides essential nutrients for a seedling, including the bran, the endosperm, and the germ. The bran protects the seed and contains B vitamins, fiber, and minerals such as iron and zinc. The endosperm provides the energy for the seed and contains carbohydrates, some protein, and few B vitamins. The germ supplies rich nourishment for the seed including B vitamins, Vitamin E, and minerals.

Nutrients are lost when grains are refined

In the United States, most of the grains in our food supply are ground and processed (***refined***) to make white flour that is then used to create many packaged foods, like white flour tortillas, saltine crackers, white bread, and sweet snacks or desserts. During this processing, **the grain's bran and the germ are removed**, leaving only the endosperm. Sometimes food companies will "enrich" these refined grains by adding back B vitamins and iron, but much of the fiber and other minerals are still lost. **This imbalance of nutrients is one of the reasons why refined grains are linked to poor physical and mental health.**

Examples of whole grains

- Oats
- Barley
- Brown rice
- Bulgur wheat
- Corn
- Popcorn
- Corn tortillas
- Whole wheat tortillas
- Quinoa
- Shredded wheat cereal
- Ingredient lists that begin with "100% whole wheat" or "whole grain flour"

Examples of Refined Grains

- White breads
- White tortillas
- Saltine and club crackers
- Donuts, cookies, snack cakes
- Most breakfast cereals unless they read 100% whole grain
- Ingredient lists that begin with "enriched wheat flour" or "wheat flour"

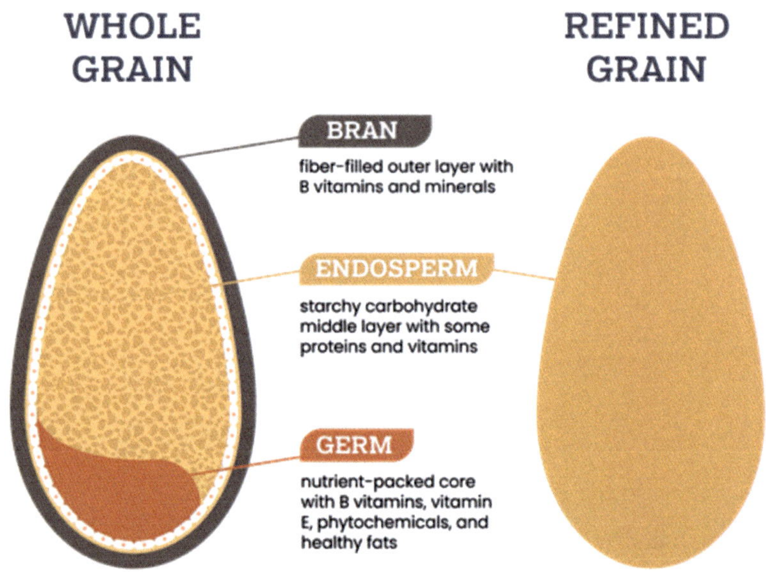

Image source: https://www.foundationhealth.org/our_community/fhp_healthbreak/the_prime_numbers_of_eating_whole_grains

Eating more whole grains may help reduce mood swings, anxiety, and depression.

Whole grains are naturally rich in an amino acid called ***tryptophan***, which helps the body make two hormones called ***serotonin*** and ***melatonin***. Serotonin, also known as the "feel good" hormone, improves mood and relaxes the brain and body. Melatonin–the "sleep" hormone–helps your body's sleep-wake cycle including your body's ability to fall asleep at night. Whole grains also help you feel full for longer and can support healthy blood sugar levels, both of which can support a healthy mood.

Studies also now show that people who eat mostly whole grains (instead of refined grains) have a lower risk for cognitive decline, dementia and Alzheimer's disease. **What are some ways that you could start including one more serving of whole grains to your meals each day?**

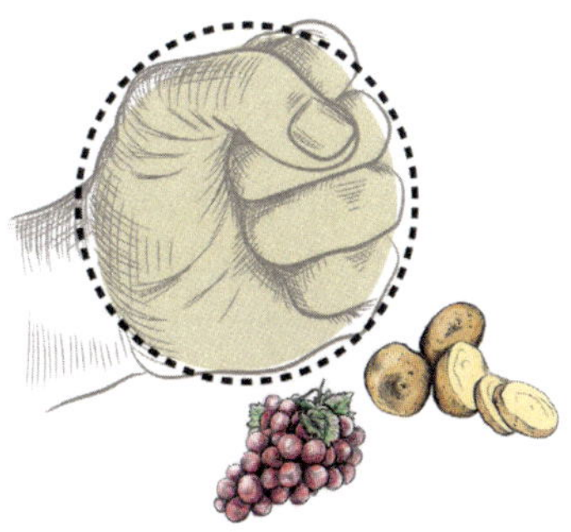

Grain Portion Size

Grain, Fruit, and Vegetable Serving (about 1/2 cup)—*fruit, cooked vegetables, beans, rice, or cereal*

Activity: Simple Steps for Making Whole Grains

New to cooking whole grains? You don't need a rice cooker or an instapot. All whole grains can be made easily using these basic steps.

1. **Place grains and water (or broth) in a pot and bring to a boil.**
2. **Reduce heat to a simmer.**
3. **Cook, covered, until tender, and most of the liquid has been absorbed.**
4. **Let stand for 5 minutes.**

Store any leftovers in the refrigerator for up to 4 days. Use as a topping for salads or combine with beans or lentils and your favorite spices for an easy meal.

Reflection: Nourishing My Second Brain

1. ***What are the things I do now to help calm myself when I am stressed? Are there any additional activities I could try to activate or "wake up" my vagus nerve to support relaxation when I need it?***

2. ***What are the things I do now to care for my microbiome? What else could I do to support it each day?***

3. Looking back at the examples of whole and refined grains on the previous page, ***where do I get grains during my day? Are these whole grains or refined grains?*** (If you aren't sure, read the ingredients label of a few of the foods you regularly eat.) ***Are these foods what my body needs to be mentally and physically healthy?***

Try It!

- ☐ To help support a healthy microbiome with probiotics, **buy a 32-ounce container of plain (unsweetened), low-fat yogurt and find new ways to eat it throughout the week.** Use it as a tangy topping for a baked potato, dip mix, or combine with oatmeal and dried fruit and chill overnight to create muesli.
- ☐ **Cook a new whole grain, such as barley, cracked wheat, or steel cut oats and take a mindful bite**. Can you see all the parts of the whole grain? What does it smell like? What flavors do you notice? How does the texture compare to white rice? Then add the cooked grain to a salad or soup. How does it affect your satiety (feeling full)?
- ☐ Read the food labels of any crackers, cereals, breads, pastas, and convenience foods that you regularly buy. If any of these are made with refined grains, **create a plan to buy a new whole grain option instead of a refined grain option the next time you are at the store.** Remember to look for 100% whole wheat or whole grain on the ingredients list.
- ☐ **Eat one portion of cooked whole grain once a day for 3-7 days as part of your daily meals and notice any changes to your digestion, sleep, or energy levels.**

NOTES

WEEK 7:
Life in Full Color

You might have heard the saying, "We eat with our eyes first."

When we see, smell, or think of food, these cues send messages to the body through the ***vagus nerve*** to prepare parts of the digestive system to get ready for eating. This stage of digestion is called the ***cephalic phase*** because it all happens in the mind.

To help illustrate this cephalic or "mental" phase of digestion, try focusing for 10 seconds on this lemon wedge. Notice all the different shades of yellow.

Can you imagine...

...how this lemon smells?

...feeling the texture of the rind?

...tasting this sour fruit?

If your mouth started watering or if your mouth puckered a bit, this was your cephalic phase of digestion in action!

EATING WITH OUR EYES

One way that we can support healthy digestion is beginning with what we see on our plate, which includes foods with bold colors

Imagine eating pesto without its green basil or chicken noodle soup without its golden carrots. Not only do colorful foods bring nutrients and flavor to our meals, they can also make them more enjoyable to eat.

Phytonutrients are special nutrients

Fruits, vegetables, and whole grains can help spark creativity in the kitchen and help to paint our plates with a rainbow of color. As an added bonus for our health, these colorful plant foods provide unique ***phytonutrients*** that animal products and refined grains can't give you. **Phytonutrients include over 4,000 different compounds that are found across all plant foods, including fruits, vegetables, beans, whole grains, herbs, spices, tea, and coffee.**

These special compounds work to protect plants from damage caused by the sun, wind, and pests and can benefit our bodies by giving us many special health advantages when we eat them. Many phytonutrients support blood vessel health and blood circulation throughout the body, including our eyes, brain, and vital organs. Other phytonutrients can help us cope with chronic stress by fighting chronic inflammation. Phytonutrients can also help stop pre-cancer cells from growing, which is one of the reasons why fruits and vegetables protect against many types of cancer.

Since there are so many different kinds of phytonutrients, the best way to get all their benefits is to eat a colorful selection of plant foods—white, yellow, orange, red, green, blue, and purple.

 *Activity: Which Colors Do I Eat Most?*

Either draw or write down the fruits and vegetables you and/or your family eat the most. What colors do you eat most often? What colors might you be overlooking or missing?

Green Foods	Red Foods

Yellow/Orange Foods	Blue/Purple Foods

White Foods	Others

Vegetables

Beets

Kidney beans

Tomato or vegetable juice

Radishes

Red bell pepper

Red onions

Red skin potatoes

Tomato

Tomato paste

Carrots

Sweet potato

Orange bell pepper

Winter squash
acorn, butternut

Yellow summer squash

Yellow bell pepper

Spaghetti squash

Bok choy

Broccoli

Brussels sprouts

Cabbage

Celery

Cilantro

Cucumber

Collards

Edamame

Green beans

Green bell pepper

Hearty green

Parsley

Peas

Romaine lettuce

Snow peas

Spinach

Sugar Snap peas

Zucchini

Eggplant

Purple cabbage

Purple potatoes

Onions

Garlic

Cauliflower

Vegetable broth

Beans - *Garbanzo, Pinto*

Lentils

Mushrooms

Potato

Fruits

Apples – *Fuji, Red Delicious*  Cranberries  Cherries  Plums  Red grapes

Raspberries  Strawberries  Watermelon

Apricot  Cantaloupe  Mango  Nectarine  Orange  Papaya  Peach  Tangerine

Apple - *Golden Delicious or Opal*  Asian pear  Banana  Lemon

Apples – *Granny Smith*  Asparagus  Avocado  Green Pear

Honeydew melon  Kiwi  Limes

Blueberries  Blackberries  Purple grapes Raisins

Prunes Plums

Applesauce Canned pears

Ready to start adding more color to your meals?

Frozen and dried fruits and vegetables are two easy options. These foods are nutritious, colorful, and can be easily added to meals or snacks.

But, most people enjoy eating fresh fruits and vegetables, too. Learning good knife skills is a great place to start when you're wanting to cook with fresh produce more often. **With more confidence knowing how to hold and use your knife, you may find that making meals with fresh fruits and vegetables:**

- Is more enjoyable
- Allows you to be more creative
- Is easier and quicker to prepare
- Offers a wider variety of texture and taste

To get you started with a safe and secure knife grip, follow these simple steps:

The most secure knife grip is with:

1. The index finger wrapped around the top of the blade, and

2. The thumb flush against the blade or handle.

3. While holding the knife with your dominant hand, curl the fingers of your other hand while cutting. Note that the knife blade is resting against the knuckles of the non-dominant hand.

4. Your index finger should not be pointed out over the blade. This grip gives you less control over the knife.

Once you've mastered this knife grip, you are now ready to begin practicing new knife cuts. Minced garlic and diced onions are two common ingredients used in recipes. It will take a little bit of practice, but working to master these skills first can help you prepare many meals more quickly, safely, and easily.

How to Dice Onions

1. Slice stem end off and discard.
2. Set onion on flat end and slice in half.
3. Remove onion peel.

4. Make a cut into the onion parallel to the board. Do not cut through the root.
5. Cutting perpendicular to the board, make thin slices into the onion.
6. Turn the onion and cut the sliced onion into cubes.
7. Hold on to the root end to keep onion intact.
8. Continue cutting until onion is completely diced.
9. Discard root end.

Want to learn more knife cuts with different types of vegetables? Visit **HowDoYouNourish.org**

Thank you to Chef Valarie Carter, MPH and the OU Culinary Medicine Program for developing this content.

Knife Cuts

As you become more comfortable with your knife, you can explore other types of ways to cut and prepare vegetables. Different cuts will affect not only how the food looks, but also its overall texture and taste!

- **Bias cut:** to cut food at an angle, especially a long vegetable, like a carrot.
- **Chiffonade:** to roll a leafy vegetable or herb and cut into strips.
- **Chop:** to cut foods into randomly shaped pieces of about the same size.
- **Dice:** to cut foods into small cubes of uniform size and shape.
- **Julienne:** to cut vegetables, fruits, or cheeses into thin strips.
- **Mince:** to chop food into extremely small randomly-shaped pieces.
- **Pare/peel:** to remove the outermost skin of a fruit or vegetable.
- **Rounds:** to cut a cylinder or cone-shaped vegetable, like carrot or zucchini, into disks.
- **Shred:** to cut or tear into small, long, narrow pieces.
- **Slice:** to cut larger pieces of food into thinner pieces, like tomatoes or onions.

How to Mince Garlic

When choosing garlic, look for plump, firm cloves enclosed in a tight, intact outer wrapper.
1
2
3

1. With the handle of the knife off the cutting board, smash cloves of garlic with the side of the knife.
2. Remove peel.
3. Chop smashed cloves into small pieces.

Reflection: Adding Color To My Life

1. ***How often were fruits and vegetables part of your meals as a child? What kinds of fruits and vegetables were served? How did that possibly shape your food preferences today? Are there any fruits or vegetables that you didn't like as a child, but that you've learned to enjoy today?***

2. Fruits and vegetables naturally grow by the seasons. Thanks to greenhouses and national food distribution systems, we can find nearly any fruit or vegetable at supermarkets just about any time of year. But, most people agree that nothing beats the taste of a fresh strawberry picked in June or tomatoes picked in August. You might have seen signs that read, "Buy local." ***Thinking back to the meaning of food in your life and what matters most to you, how might buying local fruits and vegetables support those values? If you aren't sure, check out the summary box on this page for a few possible ideas.***

Perks of Buying Local

There are many benefits to buying and eating fruits and vegetables that are grown locally.

1. **Taste**: They taste better and have stronger flavor because they are picked at their peak and get to your table in a shorter amount of time. Oftentimes produce is available to purchase within 24 hours of harvest. For the same reason, locally grown fruits and vegetables have more nutrients.
2. **Safety**:They are safer to eat because there are fewer stops between the farm and your plate.
3. **Variety:** You may discover different types of fruits and vegetables that you can't find at the grocery store. Instead of just roma tomatoes, you may find several kinds of tomatoes to choose from, like brandywine or cherokee purple!
4. **Community:** Buying local fruits and vegetables means you are supporting farmers from your community instead of sending money to big businesses outside of our state.
5. **Connection:** You may feel more connected to nature by knowing where your food was grown.

Try It! Color Challenge

- ☐ **Paint Your Plate:** Add a new color to your plate at least one time each day this week. Short on time? Try adding some dehydrated vegetables to some soup or chili, or drinking a can of vegetable juice.
- ☐ **Rainbow Shopping Basket:** While at the grocery store, buy a variety of fruits and vegetables to include at least one yellow, orange, red, green, blue/purple, and white option.
- ☐ **3 Bag Challenge:** While at the grocery store, buy 2 bags of mixed, colorful frozen vegetables, like a stir fry blend and a california blend, along with 1 bag of mixed frozen fruits, like berries. Add these to your meals throughout the week with the goal to finish all 3 bags in 7 days.

Need a few ideas to get you started with adding more color to your meals?

- » Add green lettuce (or baby spinach) and shredded carrots to a sandwich
- » Add onions and peppers to scrambled eggs, or use as filling for a breakfast burrito
- » Add onions, peppers, mushrooms, etc. to chips to make loaded veggie nachos
- » Add fresh or frozen vegetables to any noodle to make pasta primavera
- » Add frozen berries to plain yogurt and raw oats to make "overnight oats"

NOTES

WEEK 8:
Healthy Fats & Essential Proteins

"The human body then is not the solid structure issued at birth that must last until death...Rather, the human body is always in flux, more like a river- continually flowing and changing. We are renewed from what we eat..."- Roger Greenlaw, M.D.

All bodies need carbohydrates, fats, and proteins to survive. Fat is a very special nutrient that provides nourishment to our bodies in many unique ways.

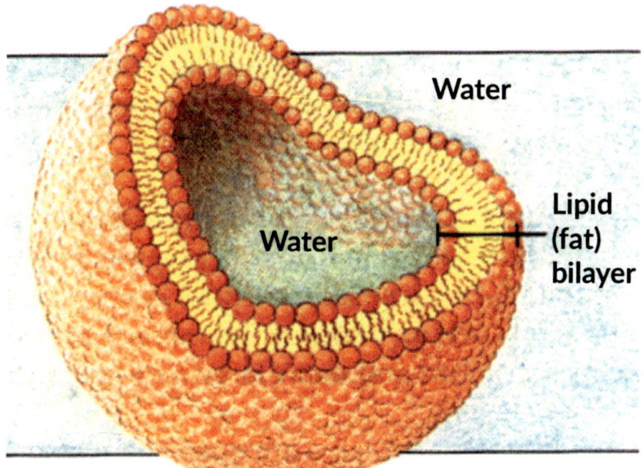

Fats help to make up the walls of every cell in our body

Image source: http://biology4alevel.blogspot.ro/2014/08/10-lipids.html

- **Flavor and Satisfaction:** Fat makes our foods more flavorful and helps us feel satisfied after a meal.
- **Fuel and Nutrient Absorption:** Fat is an important source of fuel for our bodies and is needed by the body to absorb many nutrients (vitamins A, D, E, and K and all the phytonutrients).
- **Special Messenger:** Every cell in our body needs healthy fats for their structure and communication with other cells.

More about Fat as a Special Messenger:

Fats are important building blocks of all the cells that make up our bodies. The types of fats we eat become a part of our cell walls and play a role in how our cells "talk" to one another ***(cell signaling)***, including messages to our immune system during the stress response. Omega 3 fats are known as "anti-inflammatory" while omega 6 fats are sometimes called "pro-inflammatory" because of the types of messages these fats send from cell to cell when we feel stressed. While both types of fats are needed for a healthy immune response, an imbalance of fats can cause our cells to overreact with harmful inflammatory messages when we feel stressed.

Eating a healthy balance of good fats can help support our body's ability to respond in a healthy way to stress.

Good fats can support a positive mood, better thinking and memory, healthy skin, and can even help to manage chronic pain by keeping inflammation in check. When most of our fats come from processed or refined foods, the opposite can happen: chronic inflammation can rise, we may not think or remember as clearly, depression may worsen, and chronic pain can worsen.

Healthy, essential fats can be found in many simple foods.

ESSENTIAL FATS

Activity: Oil Check

Are your cells getting the kinds of fats they need to best support your mental and physical well-being? Fats can be found in many types of foods. Take a look at the list below and mark the foods that you eat regularly.

Omega 9 (Monounsaturated fats)

EAT MOST OFTEN

- ☐ Avocados
- ☐ Olives
- ☐ Almonds
- ☐ Cashews
- ☐ Peanuts
- ☐ Peanut butter
- ☐ Pecans
- ☐ Pistachios
- ☐ Cooking oils: Olive, avocado, and canola

Omega 6 (Polyunsaturated fats)

ESSENTIAL – EAT DAILY

- ☐ Sesame seeds
- ☐ Tahini (sesame seed paste)
- ☐ Hummus (contains tahini)
- ☐ Sunflower seeds
- ☐ Sunbutter (sunflower seed butter)
- ☐ Pumpkin seeds
- ☐ Tofu
- ☐ Edamame (baby soy beans)

Omega 3 (Polyunsaturated fats)

ESSENTIAL "ANTI-INFLAMMATORY" – EAT VARIETY ONCE DAILY

- ☐ Flaxseeds
- ☐ Chia seeds
- ☐ Walnuts
- ☐ Canola oil
- ☐ Fatty fish (Sardines, mackerel, salmon)

What about cooking oils?

Avocado, canola, and olive oil are great options when cooking. You can find these oils at most grocery stores. These oils are rich in monounsaturated fats and low in saturated fat. To help protect these healthy oils from damage, store them in a dark place with the lid on tightly and cook foods at a lower temperature (medium/high or low heat instead of high heat). Once an oil starts smoking, it is unhealthy to eat. Never use an oil with a bitter taste or odor– it's rancid.

Omega 3 Fats

Omega 3 fats keep cell membranes fluid and flexible and help to soothe chronic inflammation, while helping our brains, moods, and blood vessels to be their best. **9 out of every 10 people aren't getting enough of these essential fats.** Eating fatty fish twice per week will ensure you are getting enough. If you don't care for sardines, mackerel, or salmon, you can eat one of these plant-based sources of omega 3s every day to help meet your omega 3 needs.

Saturated Fats

NOT ESSENTIAL – BEST TO LIMIT (our body makes its own saturated fat as needed)

- Butter
- Whole and 2% Milk
- Cheese
- Coconut oil
- Animal fats
- Chicken skin
- Ice cream

You can read the nutrition facts label to see how much saturated fat is in a food. The ingredients list can also help you understand which types of fats and oils are in a food.

Refined, Processed, Deep-Fried Fats

BEST TO AVOID OR LIMIT

- Stick margarine
- Foods made with "hydrogenated oils"
- Donuts, snack cakes
- Chips fried in oil
- French fries
- Packaged foods with vegetable, sunflower, safflower, soy, or corn oil ingredients

Refined Oils

When oil is deep-fried, even if the oil is a healthy option, many physical and chemical changes happen to the oil during the cooking process that take away fat's health benefits. Processed, refined, and deep fried oils are linked to depression and many physical health problems.

Reflection: Finding Balance with Essential Fats

Take a look at the foods you checked on the previous pages. What types of foods provide you with fat during your day and what types of fats are you getting from these foods? You might also find it helpful to read the ingredients label of any foods you regularly eat for "oil" ingredients. Are you eating mostly omega 9, 6, and 3 foods, or is most of the fat in your meals coming from saturated and processed/refined sources?

1. ***Looking at omega 3s specifically, are you feeding your body this essential nutrient at least several times per week?***

____

____

____

2. ***If your current fat intake appears to be imbalanced, how might eating more of these unsaturated "omega" fats help support your wellness goals?***

____

____

____

____

____

Try It! Oil Change Challenge

There are many ways to add more healthy and essential fats to your daily meals and snacks. Which of these options are you willing to try this week?

- ☐ **Switch from corn oil or vegetable oil to canola oil,** which costs about the same but gives you omega 3 fatty acids that aren't found in these other oils.
- ☐ If you enjoy the taste, **invest in a small bottle of olive oil** to enhance the flavor of sauteed vegetables or homemade salad dressings. One tablespoon per day is all you need to get the health (and taste) benefits.
- ☐ **Replace chips** or other salty snacks with a ¼ cup (small handful) of raw, roasted, or slightly salted nuts or seeds and notice any differences in how these foods affect your energy level.
- ☐ **Enjoy hummus** (a type of bean dip made with tahini or sesame seed butter) with vegetables or as a sandwich spread.
- ☐ **Spread natural peanut butter** (or other nut or seed butter) on an apple as a filling snack instead of cookies.
- ☐ **Eat an omega 3 food** every day for 7 days and notice how you feel, physically and mentally.
- ☐ **Try a meatless meal**, like a lentil or bean chili instead of beef chili.
- ☐ Something else:

____

Essential Proteins

Proteins and the essential amino acids they provide are the basic building blocks of all life. Like essential fats, protein plays many special roles in the body that are needed for our survival and well-being.

- **Food flavor.** Like fats and oils, protein foods also enhance the flavor of our meals, but in a different way. The savory (umami) or meaty flavor of foods comes from the amino acid L-glutamate.
- **Feeling full.** Eating a small amount of protein with carbohydrate-rich foods can help keep energy levels steady and our bodies feeling fuller for longer.
- **Muscle building and repair.** After digestion, proteins are broken down into amino acids, where they can be found in every cell in the human body, such as those found in our muscles and vital organs.
- **Immune function.** All of our immune cells and the antibodies they create are made up of proteins.
- **Neurotransmitter production.** Amino acids are used to make neurotransmitters. These special chemicals allow brain and nerve cells to send messages to other cells.

Proteins provide our body with essential amino acids. Each amino acid plays special roles in the body. For example, the amino acid ***L-tyrosine*** helps produce the neurotransmitter ***dopamine***, which is central to functions like memory, cognition, attention, and mood. You can find L-tyrosine in sesame seeds, soy products (like tofu), salmon, lentils, peanuts, and almonds. As another example, when we eat a protein food that contains the amino acid L-glutamate, this amino acid sends signals from the tongue to the brain to support the digestion of protein foods.

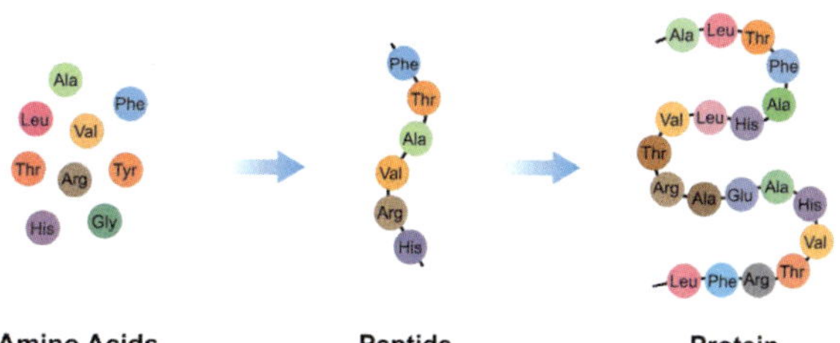

Everyone's protein needs are unique, but most of us are getting (more than) enough

Everyone's protein needs are unique and are based on age, activity level, and health conditions. In the United States, it is very rare for people to not get enough protein, and most adults eat more protein than their body needs. Lean animal proteins, like skinless chicken and fish, are nearly all protein and make it easy to quickly meet protein needs. Lentils, almonds, sunflower seeds, beans, and tofu are also great protein choices, supplying 7-12 grams of protein per serving. Unlike meats, these foods also supply healthy fats and fiber that can help you feel full, too. **To get the most out of your protein foods without overdoing it, try eating smaller amounts of protein throughout the day and consider exploring different types of protein foods, including plant-based proteins.**

Most skinless chicken breasts sold in grocery stores provide 2 full portions of protein (6-8 ounces).

Protein Portion Sizes

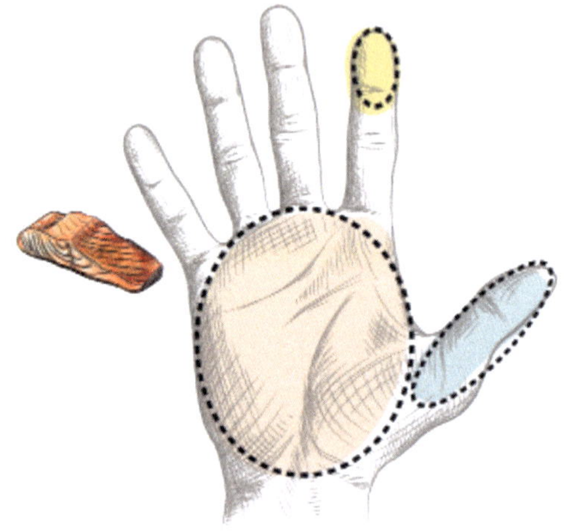

Palm
Proteins Serving (about 3-4oz) *meat; double up for vegetarian protein*

Cupped Hand
Nuts or seeds serving (about ¼ cup)

Unsalted nuts and seeds are a great source of protein, magnesium, and healthy fats–3 nutrients that all support a positive mood.

It's best to eat a variety of nuts and seeds instead of just one kind. Almonds, walnuts, pecans, cashews, and raw sunflower kernels are good choices. Natural peanut butter or sunflower seed butter (sunbutter) is also a good choice. Limit your daily serving to ¼ cup nuts/seeds or 2 Tbsp nut butter to get all the health benefits of nuts while keeping them affordable.

Building Flavor in the Kitchen with Umami

Savory (umami) is one of your five basic tastes (look back to Week 2 for more information). Meats and cheeses contain the amino acid L-glutamate, which gives these foods their savory taste. When people feel that something is "missing" from a meatless meal, it might just be that a savory ingredient is missing.

Here are a few low-cost, tasty options to help give plant-based meals a meatier kick.

Sauteed mushrooms

Garlic

Soy sauce

Nutritional yeast

Fresh, canned, roasted or sun-dried tomatoes

Nuts

REFLECTION: FINDING BALANCE WITH PROTEINS

Reflection: Finding Balance with Proteins

What types of foods provide you with protein during your day? Place a check mark by those that you regularly eat below.

Animal protein foods:

- ☐ chicken
- ☐ beef
- ☐ pork
- ☐ fish
- ☐ eggs
- ☐ milk
- ☐ cheese
- ☐ yogurt
- ☐ whey protein powder

Plant protein foods:

- ☐ beans
- ☐ lentils
- ☐ soy milk
- ☐ tofu
- ☐ tempeh
- ☐ nuts
- ☐ seeds
- ☐ peanut, nut, or seed butters
- ☐ soy, pea, or other vegan protein powder
- ☐ veggie burgers or other meat substitutes

Do you see any opportunities to add more variety to your diet? Brainstorm some ideas here.

Reflection: Finding Balance with Proteins

Most people get more of their protein from animal foods (meat, milk, eggs) than they do from plant foods (beans, lentils, nuts, seeds, whole grains). In the history of most cultures, eating meat was viewed as a status symbol for having money and power. Because it was more difficult to come by, meat was often saved for special occasions or eaten in smaller amounts. Today, meat and other animal foods are more readily available and eaten several times per day (far more often than centuries ago). Most scientists agree that this heavy demand for animal foods is harmful for the health of people and the planet for reasons like antibiotic resistance, climate change, pollution, and high risk of injury among workers.

What do you think about these historical changes? How might a heavy reliance on meat cause imbalance in our bodies? What are the benefits of saving meat for special occasions? How might plant-based proteins invite more creativity and variety to your daily meals?

Try It! Plant Protein Challenge

- ☐ **Cook dry beans or lentils from scratch:** Homemade beans and lentils often have better flavor and texture than canned. Take the time to make a pot and enjoy throughout the week.

- ☐ **Pasta makeover:** Prepare a box of high-protein pasta made with lentil or garbanzo (chickpea) flour. Follow the directions on the package carefully and keep in mind that these noodles may cook faster than regular wheat noodles. Add your favorite pasta sauce or season the noodles with a little bit of garlic and olive oil.

- ☐ **Two bean challenge:** Pick two different cans of beans to eat throughout the week, such as a can of black beans and a can of chickpeas (or pinto, kidney, navy, etc.). Think about your regular meals and new ways you can include these foods with your meals. A few ideas might be enjoying the beans cold and mixed with chopped vegetables as a colorful salad, or adding them to burger patties, meatloaf, or skillet noodle mixes.

- ☐ **Ground beef swap:** Use cooked lentils instead of ground beef in pasta sauce, as taco filling, or in casseroles.

MONTH 3: WRITING THE NEXT CHAPTER OF MY PERSONAL FOOD STORY

In this section, you are invited to explore:

» How to create a vision for being my happiest, healthiest self
» How I can find resources within my inner support circle and outside community to achieve the health goals I want
» Where I can find low-cost, nutritious foods so that I can continue supporting my mental and physical well-being

WEEK 9:
Dreaming Big, Starting Small

The human brain is designed to set goals and is capable of finding many ways to achieve the goals we want.

As you enter the last month of this initial food journey, we invite you to think about what you've learned about yourself along the way, and what additional steps you'd like to take on the road toward finding your happiest, healthiest self. As humans, we have the potential to change and grow throughout our lives. Creating new goals for ourselves can support the change and growth that we want to see, but changing habits we've held for a long time can be hard. While it can be tempting to get discouraged or to give up when we hit a roadblock, there are often other routes for reaching our desired destination if we take the time to look. It's also essential to offer ourselves ***self-compassion*** along the way.

Self-compassion can help us reach our goals

Just like mindfulness and gratitude, self-compassion is a powerful skill that can be learned through practice. Self-compassion can quiet the "all or nothing" voice we have in our heads and increase the resilient voice that says "I am worth it and I can try again". When you practice self-compassion, it can increase your motivation to continue, help you come back from mistakes, and even open your eyes to new possibilities for reaching your goals.

Self-compassion can help remind you that:

» You deserve to treat yourself with the same kindness you would give a friend when they are struggling with something difficult.

» Making mistakes or failing is part of being a human, and you are a human yourself.

» Every time you try to make changes that benefit you, you are doing this because you care for yourself, not because you are useless or unacceptable as you are.

To learn more about self-compassion and how you can build it, see the exercises in the back of this book.

Activity: Envisioning Your Happiest, Healthiest Self

With your eyes closed, picture yourself living as your happiest, healthiest self. ***What are you doing? Where are you? Who are you with? What words or images come to mind?*** Let yourself dream big even if you don't know how to achieve your dream! Make notes here.

Activity: Setting A SMART Goal

Think of one small goal for this week to move towards your happiest, healthiest self. When picking a goal, choose one that is a little challenging, but also one that you are confident you can achieve.

Use the SMART goal method:

» **Specific**—Avoid words like "more," "less" or "better."

» **Measurable**—Will you know when you've achieved it?

» **Action Based**—Not everything is in your control; make goals that you can achieve with your actions.

» **Realistic**—Choose goals you're likely to accomplish. Start small.

» **Time Frame**—Set a goal to achieve this week.

When writing your SMART goal, it can also be helpful to also state your "why." Here are a few examples:		
To help me wake up naturally without a lot of caffeine, I will greet each day with a 10 minute walk at least two days this week.	To provide my body with what it needs for a better night's rest, I will put away all electronics by 10:00 pm and avoid caffeine in the afternoon for at least three days this week.	To support my mental well-being, I will experiment with a new recipe this week that has an omega 3 ingredient, such as flax, chia, or fish.
To help relax my body, I will eat mindfully during three meals this week without distractions (avoiding phone, TV, tablet).	To support the health of the cells that make up my body, I will include one healthy source of fats with at least one meal or snack each day this week, such as nuts, seeds, avocado, or olive oil.	To fight fatigue more naturally, I will choose water or unsweetened tea instead of a soda or sweet tea at least one time each day this week.
		To nurture my resilience to stress, I will practice one mindfulness, self-compassion, or gratitude exercise each day this week, including any of the activities in the back of this book.

Write your SMART goal here:

Why is this goal important to you? What bigger change or benefit will meeting this goal provide? How confident are you that you will complete your goal? (If you aren't feeling very confident, try breaking your goal into smaller steps that are more achievable.)

REFLECTION & TRY IT: MAKING A ROAD MAP

Reflection: Making a Road Map

Bill wants to change his diet after his doctor told him he has prediabetes. He throws away all of his favorite, "unhealthy" snacks and replaces all of them with foods he doesn't usually eat. Monday and Tuesday he does great, by Wednesday he's getting tired of his new foods and he's pretty hungry when he goes to bed. On Thursday, he's tired of all this new food and is starving, so he picks up two taquitos and a hot dog at the convenience store nearby. It tastes good, but he is mad at himself for not being able to stick with his new eating plan. Friday he goes shopping again with the few grocery dollars he has left, and decides to buy his old food choices because he already tried to eat healthy and failed.

After reading this scenario, do you think Bill's goals were realistic and achievable? What are some things that Bill could try differently that could set himself up for success in the future? For example: How might he approach goal setting next time? Do you think the "why" behind his goal was enough? Is Bill being self-compassionate? How could self-compassion help Bill be more successful?

Try It! Starting Your Journey

- ☐ **Set a small goal that you can accomplish this wee**k that supports your journey to your happiest, healthiest self. Write your goal down and place it somewhere that you can see it.
- ☐ **Take a look at the self-compassion section** that is located in the back of this book, beginning on page 155. Choose at least one exercise and try it. Repeat the exercise anytime you find yourself feeling frustrated this week.
- ☐ **At the end of the week, did you meet your goal?** If you did, recommit to the goal for another week to help create a new habit. If you didn't meet your goal, think about Bill's story above. What can you do differently to set yourself up for success next week?

WEEK 10:
Nourishment From My Inner Circle

"I lied and said I was busy.
I was busy;

but not in a way most people understand.

I was busy taking deeper breaths.
I was busy silencing irrational thoughts.
I was busy calming a racing heart.
I was busy telling myself I am okay.

Sometimes, this is my busy -
and I will not apologize for it."

– Brittin Oakman

Our bodies need and deserve self-care

Food can bring meaning to our lives, feed our happiness in different ways, and support our resilience against the stressors in life. As we've already explored, food can be an important part of how we care for and express ourselves.

But, our bodies need more than nutritious food to thrive. Our bodies are designed to give us signs when we need more self-care. **Have you experienced any of these lately?**

» Fatigue or lack of energy

» Irritability, impatience, anger

» Feeling busy, but not feeling accomplished

» Difficulty concentrating or remembering

» Feeling like the only one who can help everyone

When we are feeling this way, there are many things we can do to reset (or at least improve) how we are feeling. **These things can be found in five different "self-care buckets" that we can draw from:**

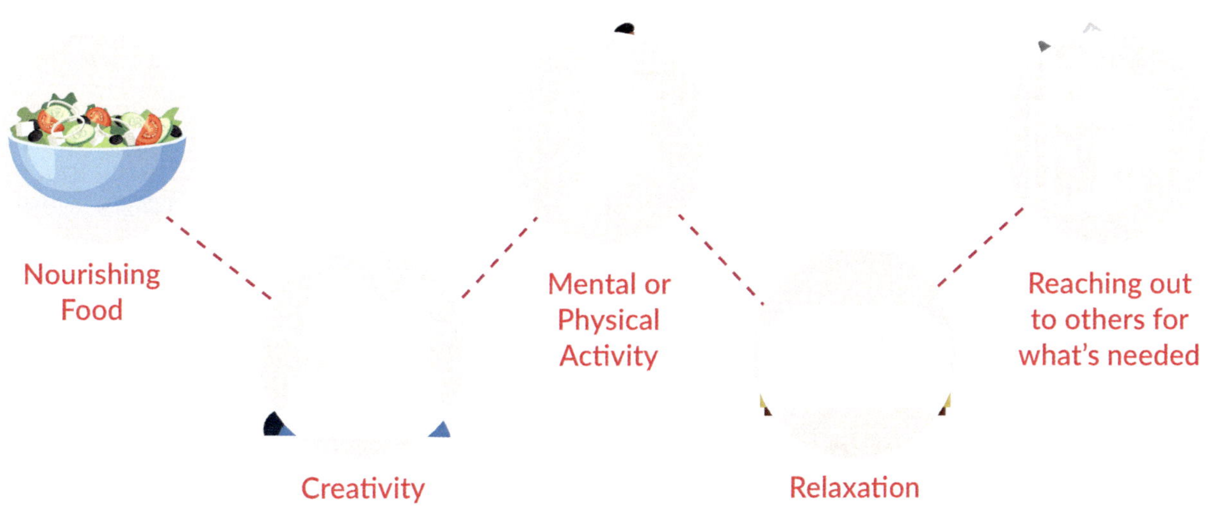

WHAT DOES HUNGRY FEEL LIKE?

Can You Relate?

"If I get bored or depressed, I tear the house down... and then I'm mad at myself for doing that because then I'm bloated, and I feel miserable and I'm like, 'why am I doing this?' "

Can You Relate?

"When you're feeling kinda depressed, eating might make you feel better for the moment, but it's not going to make you feel better later. Sometimes I end up eating until it makes me sick, and then it's like, 'oh, that was a mistake.'"

Sometimes when our body is craving self-care, the first thing we might turn to is food.

Foods that are high in sugar, salt, and fat can help soothe our stress for the moment (see week 3 for more information). Many of these foods are cheap and easy to find, so they can quickly become our first "go to" anytime we need to release some stress. When stress is guiding our food choices, we can lose connection with our body's natural hunger and satiety (fullness) cues.

The ***hunger and fullness scale*** is one tool that we can use to check-in with our body before we turn to food. Read each point on the scale below from 1 through 10, where 1 is extremely hungry and 10 is painfully full.

Hunger-Fullness Scale:

10	Extremely stuffed, nauseous
9	Stuffed, very uncomfortable
8	Overfull, somewhat uncomfortable
7	Full but not uncomfortable, food may not taste as good as it did initially
6	Satisfied, but could eat a little more
5	Starting to feel hungry
4	Hungry, stomach growling
3	Uncomfortably hungry, distracted, irritable
2	Very hungry, low energy, weak and dizzy
1	Starving, no energy, very weak

Knowing when it's time to stop: When you begin to feel satisfied or full (6 to 7 range), that's the time to stop eating. When you find yourself wanting to eat after you've reached a 6 or 7, that's a great time to check-in and ask yourself, "What else does my body need right now besides food?" or "What would be better than food at this moment?" This is when your other self-care buckets can come into play (see next page).

Knowing when it's time to eat: When your body is sending you signals that you are hungry (4 to 5 range), that's a good time to feed your body nourishing food. Not everyone experiences hunger in the same way. Some people may forget to eat when they are stressed because they don't experience typical hunger pangs. Instead, feelings of low energy, weakness, and dizziness (1 to 3) may be important signs that our body is not getting the nutrition it needs.

Activity: Filling My Buckets

Thinking back to the self-care buckets that we introduced on page 117, create your own self-care list. These activities include things you can do to nourish yourself at times when you aren't physically hungry for food. Try to fill each bucket with at least two options.

Creativity	Mental or Physical Activity	Relaxation	Reaching out to Others

If you don't know where to begin, here are a few ideas to help you get started:

- Work on a puzzle
- Call a friend
- Doodle or draw
- Stretch
- Create a playlist or listen to music
- Use a coloring book
- Go for a walk or exercise
- Sing
- Spend time with your pet
- Journal
- Deep breathing, mindfulness, or meditation

REFLECTION: FINDING MY NOURISHMENT

Reflection: Finding My Nourishment

In Week 3, we explored how food and stress are related. For this week's reflection, use this space to create a self-care plan for times when you are feeling stressed.

Can You Relate?

"I definitely like to eat when I'm sad or when I'm depressed. I eat a lot when I'm tired...I battle that with the rational side of me that knows better, that knows I should be eating healthier and should be eating proteins and vegetables ... If I'm winning the battle, I'll be eating better and making better choices. If I'm losing the battle, then I'm eating things that are more sweets and that kind of stuff, so it just depends on how well the rest of my coping skills are working at that time."

1. ***How does stress affect your food choices? Do you find yourself not eating, even though your body might be sending you signals to eat? Or, do you find yourself eating when you are not hungry? What types of meals or snacks do you choose to eat when you are stressed?***

2. Next, imagine yourself practicing some self-care activities during this time to ease your stress. ***Which activities or bucket of activities came to mind?***

3. Now, make a plan for what step(s) you will take the next time you are feeling stressed that will provide your body with the self-care it needs.

4. *What are the physical feelings (or numbers on the Hunger-Fullness scale) you will be checking for to let you know if your body is hungry for nourishing food and if it is hungry for other kinds of self-care?*

5. *If your body is hungry for food, what are some meals or snacks that will nourish you? What will you eat if you are short on time or not feeling well?*

6. *If your body is not hungry for food, what are some self-care activities that will help? What can you do if you are short on time or not feeling well? (Check back to the previous activity for some ideas.)*

WEEK 11:
Nourishment From My Community

Communities can be described in different ways, including people who live in the same place or people who share common interests, life experiences, or values.

While we can't always choose where we live, we can find nourishment within other communities that we choose to join. These types of communities can help strengthen our resilience and provide us with an opportunity to give back to others. **Whether it's an online support group, volunteer group, AA or NA group, cooking club, weekly trip to the farmers' market, or something else, our "communities of choice" can help remind and support us in those values that we want to express and the direction that we want to go.** If we can't find what we are needing in one community, it might be time to explore other groups or organizations that can help to bring more meaning, resources, purpose, or joy in our lives.

Below are different types of communities and some of the benefits associated with being a part of each kind of community.

Support Groups

Grief/loss, alcoholic anonymous (AA), narcotics anonymous (NA), survivors of domestic abuse: *Improve depression, boost motivation and hope*

Which type(s) of community can help nourish you and allow you to nourish others in return?

Volunteer Groups

Humane society, Reading Partners, assistance league, Big Brothers and Big Sisters: *Boost self-confidence and self-esteem, improve depression, learn new skills, connect with your community*

Advocacy Groups

Food justice, environment/climate justice, voting rights, 2SLGBTQIA+ rights: *Connect with others with shared values, amplify your voice and impact*

Fitness or Sports Groups

Local YMCA or YWCA, recreational leagues, walking or running clubs, bike club: *Improve physical fitness and mental well-being, connect with others and build relationships, develop teamwork skills, reduce stress, boost energy*

Creative Arts

Sewing clubs, acting groups, photography clubs, book clubs, writing circles: *Reduce stress, increase positive emotions, learn and strengthen skills, increase self-confidence.*

Activity: Visualizing My Community of Choice with an Ecomap

Sometimes it can be hard to appreciate all of the current and potential sources of support and strength within your community. Making an ***ecomap*** can help you to identify all of the important relationships in your life that form your support network. An ecomap can also help you better see gaps in your network that you might want to find and fill through new relationships. Any time you are faced with a challenge, you can turn to your ecomap to help you identify people and resources in your social circle that might be best to support you.

Creating an ecomap is simple:

1. Write your name in the center circle.
2. In the smaller circles, add the groups or people that make up your community of choice. These could include any of the groups listed on the previous page, family members, friends, co-workers, classmates, religious affiliations, or any other groups that are important in your life. Use a line to connect each circle to you.
3. You can also use the Ecomap to list out any groups or connections you'd like to create. Write each idea in an empty circle. You can add a connection line after that relationship is established.

Here is an example:

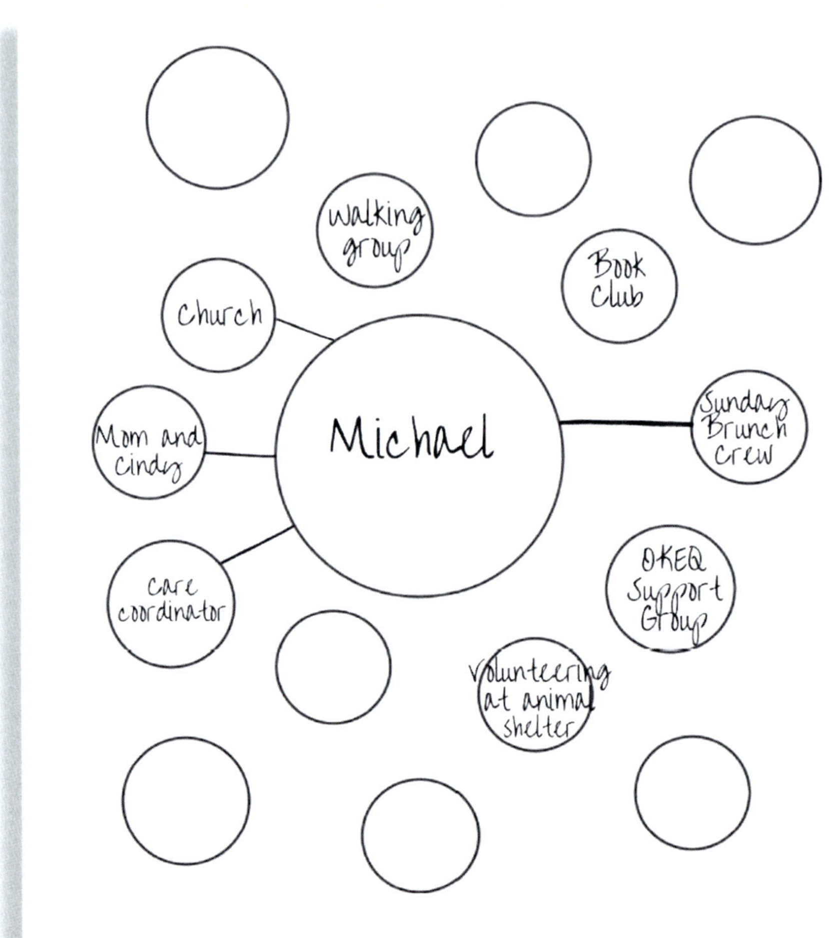

My Ecomap

LOW-COST NUTRITION IN YOUR COMMUNITY

Throughout this book, we've explored some of the different ways that food can help you connect with your deeper values. Most of these pages have encouraged you to look within yourself to discover more about what is important to you and how nourishing foods can support you in your life journey. **Now, let's explore some of the places where you can find nourishing foods as you move forward in your food journey.**

There are many simple, inexpensive foods that can help support a healthy body and mind that cost less than 50 cents a day. Even including one or two of these foods as part of your daily meals can make a big impact on how you feel. Here are just a few examples of these low-cost superstars. ***Which of these might you add to your regular shopping list?***

1 cup of cooked lentils

21 cents

1 cup of cooked oatmeal

25 cents

1 teaspoon of spices

4 cents

½ onion

24 cents

1 large carrot

16 cents

½ cup of canned beans

30 cents

½ cup frozen mixed vegetables

31 cents

1 tea bag

17 cents

1 banana

30 cents

1 handful of sunflower seeds

23 cents

¼ cup mixed dried fruit

50 cents

Something else: ____________

__ cents

 *Special Note*

For many communities, healthy food options are limited. To solve this problem, each community can come together to advocate for and build access to the foods they want. There are many organizations that are working with communities to help improve people's access to nutritious foods. If this kind of work inspires you, now might be a good time in your life to get involved! You can visit HowDoYouNourish.org to learn more.

Activity: Dollar Store Finds

There are many nourishing food staples that can be found at dollar stores! *Can you find some of the possibilities in this word search?*

- ☐ Tuna
- ☐ Salmon
- ☐ Chicken
- ☐ Sardines
- ☐ Black Tea
- ☐ Green Tea
- ☐ Beans
- ☐ Lentils
- ☐ Sunflower Seeds
- ☐ Walnuts
- ☐ Spices
- ☐ Whole Wheat Bread
- ☐ Brown Rice
- ☐ Oatmeal
- ☐ Raisin Bran

B R O W N R I C E S Q J Q W P Q U S L S
V S U N F L O W E R S E E D S H P J S A
T F Y B R V T N W A L N U T S U M L R L
L I Q J F T U R A I S I N B R A N W G M
S N Y H W V N L R U L U Q D N Z S M S O
E X Q R B E A N S A X M X H H Y R J P N
O J S Y C C H I C K E N T F R U X A I A
G W H O L E W H E A T B R E A D A J C W
R X L T V M P H H R N E L S B V R I E K
E S A R D I N E S V M P E G J J A C S K
E U B L A C K T E A E X N B Q V I P C F
N F A E T W C U T M R D T C P E S B I A
T M E W M L I I M F R S I P P V I L A Y
E O A T M E A L G F H S L A C W N Y T W
A O Y G P T U O R P T I S S E I S E Z T

If your current food budget needs a boost, here are a few options to consider:

Hunger Free OK SNAP Hotline

Not sure if you qualify for the **Supplemental Nutrition Assistance Program (SNAP)**? Don't know how to apply? Call the SNAP Hotline and apply in 30 minutes or less: (877) 760-0114 (Mon-Fri, 8 am-8 pm).

Or, you can visit: hungerfreeok.org/resources/snap/

Double Up Oklahoma

Already have SNAP? **Double Up Oklahoma (DUO)** can provide you with extra DUO bucks to spend on fresh fruits and vegetables. When you shop at participating grocery stores and farmers markets, simply spend a SNAP dollar on SNAP-eligible purchases and get a matching DUO dollar to spend on fruits and veggies, up to $20 per day.

Find out more and find participating retailers by visiting: doubleupoklahoma.org/

Food Pantries

Food pantries often rely on donations, but more and more locations are offering fresh produce and other healthy shelf-stable foods. Most food bank websites allow you to search for food pantries and other free food near you.

For a listing of food pantries in the ***Tulsa and eastern Oklahoma*** *areas:* https://okfoodbank.org/find-food/

For a listing of food pantries in the ***Oklahoma City and western Oklahoma*** *areas:* https://www.regionalfoodbank.org/get-help/

Reflection: My Community of Choice

1. Describe the different communities where you belong. ***What sources of strength do these communities provide to you? How might joining additional communities support you in reaching your goals?*** If you need some ideas, look back to the first page of this section.

2. ***What do you think is the biggest food or nutrition problem facing your community? What can you do to help your community become healthier or improve its vitality?*** Remember to dream big, but start small with one realistic, achievable step you could take this week.

NOTES

WEEK 12:
Revisiting Meaning of Food in Life and Wrap Up

"Change is not an event, it's a process." - Cheryl James

What's Changed?

As you are nearing completion of this workbook, we invite you to revisit the results from your **"Meaning of Food in Life" survey** that you took at the beginning of this program.

- Do you see food ***any differently*** now? If so, how?
- If you took the survey again, would your ***results change***? If so, how would they change?
- What have you ***discovered*** about yourself over the past 12 weeks?
- Where are you ***headed next*** in your journey to better nourishment?

Creating a Wellness Vision

A wellness vision is a compelling plan for doing the kinds of self-care and other positive habits you want in your life. You started to develop a wellness vision several weeks ago when you drew your "happiest, healthiest" self. Before then, you've taken additional steps on this journey by trying new foods, completing new activities, and answering reflection questions in this book. Taking all of these things together, you are now ready to create a wellness vision, which can either be written as a letter to your future self or expressed creatively through a vision board. In this final section, you are invited to create both of these.

Activity: Planning Your Vision Board

A ***vision board*** is a collage of images and words representing your wellness goals or dreams.

What do you want represented in your vision board?

To get started, think about what you would look and feel like at your ideal level of "whole person" wellness. Remember, bodies come in all shapes and sizes. Focus on those things that are in your control as you reflect on the following questions:

1. ***What kind of person do you want to be when it comes to your health, physical and mental fitness, or wellness?***

2. ***What are the most important parts of this vision?***

3. ***What have been your best experiences so far with the key parts of this vision...what times have you felt fully alive and present?*** Describe one of these experiences.

4. ***What do you value most about your life? How can your wellness vision support these values?***

5. *What makes this vision really important to you? Why do you want to reach this vision?*

6. *What strengths can you draw on to help you realize your vision and meet your goals?*

7. *What challenges, roadblocks, or detours do you expect having to work through on the way to reaching your vision? How can you plan for those? How can your strengths help you overcome your challenges?*

8. *What self-care skills, such as appreciating the present moment (mindfulness), gratitude, or self-compassion, can help you realize your vision and meet your challenges?*

Remember, a vision board is meant to recognize that as humans, we are constantly growing and changing and will need different kinds of support as we move through these changes. It is meant to be a reminder that regardless of where we are in life, we are worthy of being the happiest, healthiest version of ourselves, both now and in the future

Activity: Making Your Vision Board

1. After you have reflected on what you want in your wellness vision, start gathering materials to create your vision board. Start looking through magazines or online for words or pictures that illustrate parts of your vision. Print or clip pictures or words that represent your vision and place them in a pile.

2. Arrange the words and pictures on a piece of cardboard or poster board. Some people like to organize their pictures and words by themes or by goals. For example, if you would like to start walking, you could organize images and words together that illustrate this goal. Other people may prefer to mix up the images and words. Either way is fine.

3 Place a picture of yourself or something that represents you in the middle of the board, so you are at the center of your vision.

5 Hang your vision board in a place where you will see it every day. This should be an area in your home where you spend a lot of time or walk by each day, such as the back of your bedroom door or the refrigerator.

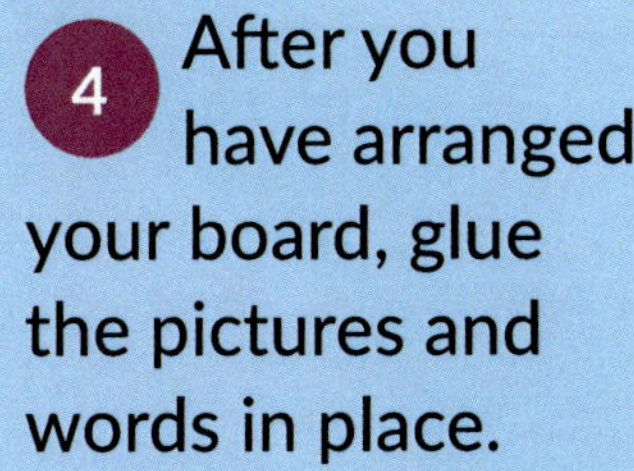

4 After you have arranged your board, glue the pictures and words in place.

6 Look at your board each day as a reminder of your wellness vision. Your vision board can be updated by replacing or adding new images whenever needed.

Looking for something fun to do with a friend or family member? This activity can be done alone or together!

TRY IT! A LETTER TO MY FUTURE SELF

Activity: Writing a Letter to Your Future Self

As you end this part of your food journey and prepare to start a new chapter, we invite you to write a letter to your future self. You can turn back to this letter anytime you need some self-support, motivation, hope, or encouragement to stay focused on achieving your goals. Here are a few steps that you can use as a guide to help you write your letter. We've also included an example letter on the next page.

Steps for writing your letter

1. ***Find an inspiring space for writing and reflection.***
   - Can you add any relaxing elements to this writing space, like quiet music or scents, or even take your experience outside in nature (if that is a calming place for you)?

2. ***Start your letter by addressing it to your future self. Be sure to include the date you write the letter to remind your future self of when you wrote it.***
   - If you'd like, set a specific timeframe for when you would like to open this letter. For example, you can write for 1 year, 5 years, or even a decade in the future.

3. ***Reflect on the present. Think about what is happening in your life right now and how you are feeling. Explore your strengths and areas for growth. Use this time to gain clarity about what you want to accomplish and the person you want to be.*** Here are some questions that might help you:
   - What is working in my life right now? What is not?
   - Where am I putting my energy? What is boosting my energy? Is there anything that drains my energy?
   - What is surprising me about the present?
   - What have I accomplished? What are the lessons I have learned?

4. ***Set your intentions and goals for the timeframe you are writing for. Imagine the steps you will need to take before reaching your goal and write them down.***
   - What will the future look like when I reach my goals?

5. ***Write about your hopes and dreams for the future. Let your feelings flow as you share your hopes, fears, and dreams. Express yourself with authenticity and vulnerability- this letter is a space that is free from judgment.***
   - What are the possibilities I dream for myself?
   - What am I looking forward to?
   - If I could have everything I wanted, what would it look like?

6. ***Sign the letter and seal it. Find a special place to keep it until you decide to open it.***

Be sure to add some of your favorite quotes, inside jokes, or favorite things to make your future self smile or laugh!

Writing a letter to your future self can be a powerful activity to help you imagine what is possible in your life. Remember, we are all worthy of happiness...let this letter be a reminder to you of that!

April 1, 2024

Dear future me,

If you are reading this, it means that I remembered and kept this letter in a safe place. Way to go, me (you)? I'm writing this because I am trying to make some changes in my life and I'm not quite sure how things will turn out.

Right now, I'm sitting at home in that old blue chair that Steve thinks is ugly, but we know is the most comfortable. Shadow is snuggled up next to me, so I thought now would be the best time to write. I have been feeling extra tired and achy lately and I've been wanting to do what I can to feel better. I haven't been sleeping well, it's hot in the bedroom and I can't stop my mind from racing. Over the last few months, I've started making some changes that are helping. I've been walking around the block or taking a few deep breaths when I start feeling too stressed out. I'm proud of myself for keeping up with these new things.

I hope that when you read this letter, you've found even more things that help you feel good. Maybe you've worked up to taking a 30 minute walk on most days of the week. I am hoping you can now touch your toes because you tried (and learned to enjoy) yoga! Maybe now that you are feeling better, you are back to cooking at home more (at least most days of the week). You have always loved to cook, but haven't been so good at the planning and shopping part. Now, I hope you have come to enjoy grocery shopping because your knees don't hurt as much. I can imagine you sitting around the table with friends enjoying spaghetti and Mom's special sauce (that you have hopefully perfected).

I hope you are speaking kinder to yourself and are practicing more self-compassion. Remember "the privilege of a lifetime is being who you are." Continue using your affirmations! Hopefully you are surrounded by people who love and care for you and have left relationships that don't bring happiness into your life.

It's time for the Wheel to start, so I better sign off for now. Is Vanna still there after Pat retired?

Good bye for now, and best wishes. Keep hanging in there!

With love and hope,

Me

APPENDIX

The following resources are designed to support you in your food journey:

» Self-Care Exercises
» Food Bundles
» Recipes
» Meaning of Food in Life Questionnaire
» References

SELF-CARE EXERCISES

MINDFULNESS

Exercises in this section:

- Soup Bowl Breathing
- 5-4-3-2-1
- Mindful Cup of Tea
- Nature's Anchor

Listen to these activities here:

Past, future, and present: What is mindfulness and what does it have to do with food?

As humans, we can spend a lot of our time thinking about things that have happened in the past or are coming up in the future. Sometimes these thoughts may help to bring us peace, like thinking back on a cherished memory, or these thoughts can help us feel excited or optimistic, like when we are looking forward to seeing an old friend. **But, when we repeatedly think about unpleasant memories or unwanted possibilities, these thoughts can be stressful and even prevent us from focusing on the things we need or want to get done.**

Mindfulness is the simple (but not always easy) practice of re-focusing your mind's attention to the present moment. Mindfulness is being aware of how you are feeling and what you are sensing right now, without judgment. Practicing mindfulness can help decrease stress, improve concentration, and help to better manage emotions. When it comes to food, **mindfulness can help us reconnect with our physical body** so we will be more likely to eat when we are hungry, get more satisfaction and nourishment from our meals without judging ourselves, and stop eating when we are full.

Like any kind of new exercise, mindfulness exercises can be challenging at first. It is very common and normal for thoughts about the past and the future to come up while trying a new mindfulness exercise. Every time a new thought emerges, this is a new opportunity to practice setting the thought aside and re-focusing on your chosen exercise.

Mindful eating is a great place to start practicing mindfulness because it encourages you to use all 5 senses to enjoy the food you are eating and think about the food in different ways. For example, where did the food come from? Who grew the food? How was it prepared? As you become more aware of the food you eat and how you feel while eating, you may find yourself reaching for different types of food (see more in week 2, page 31). Mindful eating also tells your body to switch to the "rest and digest" mode (See more in week 3, page 35).

Mindful eating is only one type of mindfulness exercise. We invite you to experiment with the following mindfulness exercises at different times throughout the week to see which ones work best for you.

SOUP BOWL BREATHING

☐ *Yes! I tried this exercise*

Time: 90 seconds

When you need to clear your mind, de-stress, get focused, or wind down, try this exercise.

1. Think of your favorite soup.
2. Gently cup your hands like you are holding your favorite soup. You can also just put your hands down in your lap. Sit up tall, like your spine was made of a stack of pennies, with both feet on the floor. Close your eyes or glance down.
3. Imagine breathing in like you are smelling a delicious bowl of soup, and breathing out like you are blowing on it to cool down—carefully so as not to splash soup everywhere!
4. Breathe in for four seconds.
5. Breathe out for eight seconds.
6. Repeat three times.

Reflection: ***How did your physical body feel immediately after completing this activity? How did your mind feel? Is this activity something that you think would be helpful when you feel stressed?***

☐ *Yes! I tried this exercise*

Time: 3-5 minutes

Do you need a ritual to connect with your mind, body, or spirit? Try this one whenever you need it.

Put your feet flat on the ground.

Silently, to yourself, name **five things you can see in the room...**

Now name **four things you can hear in the room...**

Next, name **three sensations you feel in your body...**

Then, name **two things you can smell...**

And finally, [pick **one thing** to consider from the list below]

» ...one thing for which you are grateful.
» ...one thing that inspires you.
» ...one person you appreciate.
» ...one wish for the world.
» ...one hope or dream for yourself.
» ...one good quality about yourself.

Reflection: ***How did using all five senses affect your feelings of connection with.. Your mind? Your body? Your spirit?***

MINDFUL CUP OF TEA

☐ *Yes! I tried this exercise*

Time: 5-10 minutes

1. Pick a tea that speaks to you. Do you need to relax? Try chamomile or herbal tea. Need to add some pep to your step? Try green tea, ginger tea, or fruity option.

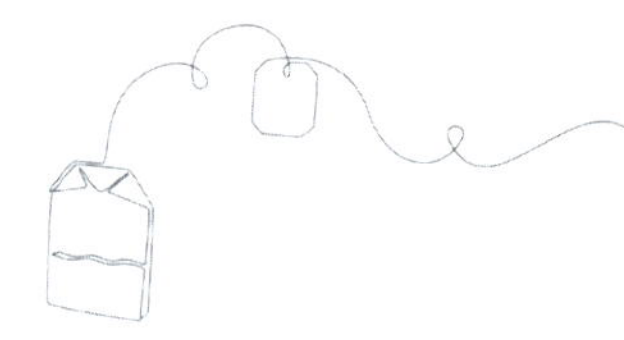

2. Find a space to enjoy your tea. Ideally, this is a quiet space away from work or your daily routine.

3. Put the tea into your cup and pour the hot water over it. As the water meets the tea, watch how the color swirls and deepens.

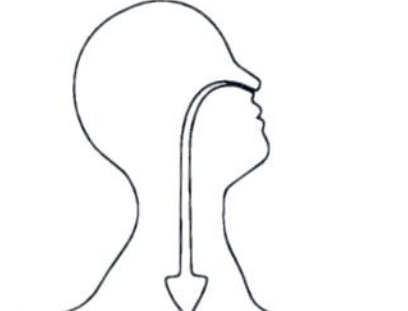

4. As your tea brews, take a few mindful breaths: Inhale for 3 seconds, hold it for 2 seconds, exhale for 3 seconds, and hold it for 2 seconds. Lift your head while exhaling and relax as you exhale.

5. Now hold the cup in your hands, look at the colors and see how the light reflects off the surface. Does your mouth feel like it wants to take a drink? What do you smell?

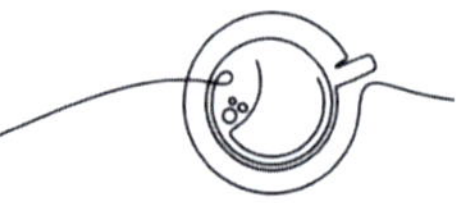

6. Bring the cup up to your lips. Can you feel the warmth from the steam on your face? Does the cup feel warm in your hands? Take a slow sip and savor the tea. Have you tasted this before? Are there any layers to the flavor? Take a few breaths between each drink to stay anchored in these mindful moments.

7. As you drink slowly, continue to focus on the tea. Your mind may wander, that is okay. Maybe you are wondering what the point of this activity is, notice the thought, and go back to your tea. Just bring your thoughts back to your tea.

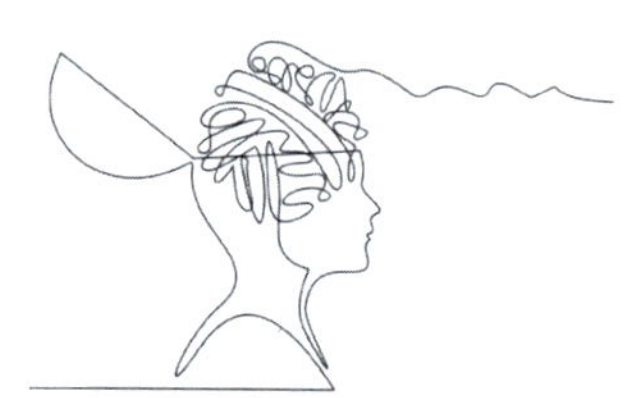

8. Look deeply into the cup, you may see sunshine or rain that helped grow the tea, or the farmers who grew the tea, or even the truck drivers and all the people that were involved in bringing this cup of tea to your hands.

9. As you continue to drink your cup of tea, express gratitude to yourself for taking a moment out of your busy day to take care of yourself.

***Reflection:* Did you find it hard to stay focused on the tea? How does your body now feel after drinking your tea?**

Adapted from Dragonfly Tea. How to Press Pause with a Little 'Tea Mindfulness'. Dragonfly Tea Blog. Published October 12, 2021. Accessed March 4, 2024. https://dragonflytea.com/blogs/our-blog/tea-mindfulness

NATURE'S ANCHOR

☐ *Yes! I tried this exercise*

Time: 5 minutes

This simple exercise can be done with any small natural object like a stone, acorn, or seashell.

1. Begin by carefully looking at your item. Pay close attention to the colors in the item, how vivid or soft are they? How does the light reflect on the surface? Do you notice any patterns?
2. Roll the item in your hand or between your fingers. What is the texture of the item? Does it feel smooth or rough? Is it cold or warm?
3. Focus deeply on the experience of holding the special item. Appreciate all the things that make this item unique.
4. While fully focusing on your item, let go of stress or regret, or pressure from the past or future. You are present with your special stone.

Just like a worry stone, you can keep your stone or other small item with you and rub it with your fingers when you feel overwhelmed with emotions to help to anchor you to the present.

Reflection: ***What did you appreciate about your item that you hadn't noticed before? What was it like to focus on each part of the item? When did your mind wander? What moments of beauty might be unnoticed in your life?***

Exercise adapted from "Here and Now Stone" exercise developed by Neff K, Germer C. The Mindful Self-Compassion Workbook: A Proven Way to Accept Yourself, Build Inner Strength, and Thrive. The Guilford Press; 2018

SELF-CARE EXERCISES

SELF-COMPASSION

Exercises in this section:

- » Warm Embrace
- » Suncatchers
- » Create Your Own Affirmation
- » Safe and Secure

Listen to these activities here:

What is self-compassion and what does it have to do with food?

We all have probably shown compassion for someone else at one time or another. **Compassion** is more than a feeling, it's an action that we take when we see someone else who is experiencing some type of emotional or physical pain. We show compassion for others when we take time to connect with their suffering and provide some kind of emotional support or physical help.

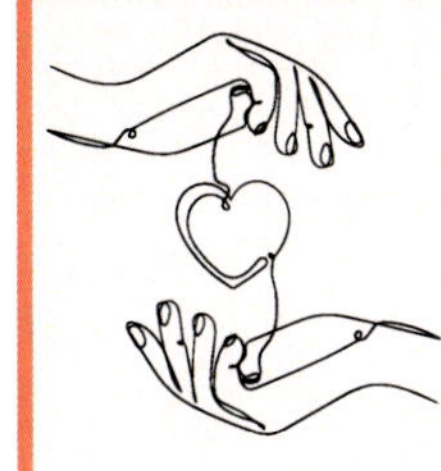

Compassion: Seeing the suffering of others ***and*** then taking action to help.

Self-compassion means treating yourself with the same kindness and comfort that you would offer to someone else when you fail at something, make a mistake, or feel inadequate. Instead of thinking about ourselves harshly, we respond by offering ourselves supporting words and other forms of self-care.

Self-Compassion: Turning compassion inward ***to yourself*** when you fail, make mistakes, or feel inadequate.

When you are trying to make a change to become your happiest and healthiest self, there will be times when you don't quite reach your goals, even if the goal is small and "easy." For example, let's say you try to make a new recipe, and you accidentally burn it because you weren't paying close enough attention. Or, you meant to buy the healthier option at the grocery store and got home to find that you bought the wrong thing.

These are times when self-compassion can make all the difference in where your journey leads. Take a moment to remember that your desire or attempt to change came from a place of caring for yourself, rather than turning your attention to how you failed. Having self-compassion means you accept yourself as a human, and all of the mistakes and frustration that comes with the human experience. The more you open your heart to this idea, the more you can grow compassion for yourself and others.

Having self-compassion on your food journey can help you to keep going after setbacks or frustration, help you stay motivated, and not give up. Treating yourself with self-compassion will make it easier to explore new and different ways of making the changes that you want if your first attempt doesn't work out. It will open doors to learning new skills and sticking to the new habits you want to create.

Don't know where to start? Try some of the following exercises to strengthen your self-compassion "muscles" and repeat them as many times as you need throughout your food journey.

WARM EMBRACE

☐ *Yes! I tried this exercise*

 *Time: 1 minute*

We are social creatures and giving yourself a warm embrace is one way to comfort and calm yourself when you are feeling down. This practice might feel silly at first, but you can think of it like eating a bowl of warm soup on a cold day. Just like being hugged by a loved one, the physical touch from a self-hug can release a hormone called oxytocin, which helps us to feel positive emotions like peace and trust. This is the same hormone that is released when you snuggle up with a partner, furry friend, or a soft pillow and blanket.

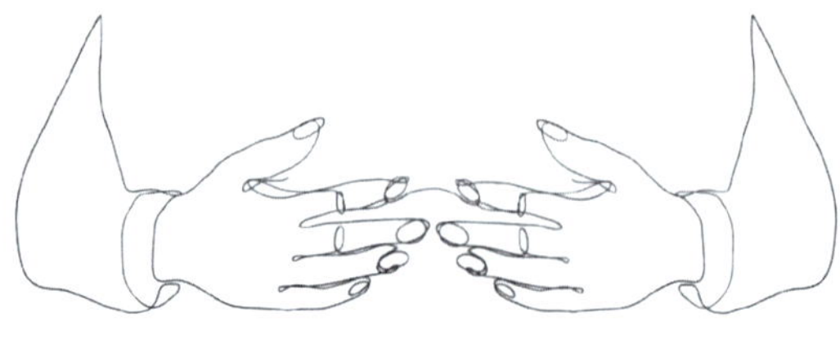

If you are upset, stressed, or sad, try giving yourself a warm embrace. This can be done in different ways, such as gently touching your cheek or arm, or slowly rocking your body. If you are around other people, you can just fold your arms and give yourself a small comforting squeeze. If that doesn't feel right, just think about giving yourself a big, warm embrace.

Try doing this simple warm embrace a few times a day for at least a week. Hopefully this will create a new habit of being kind to yourself through physical touch.

 *Reflection:* ***Think about how your body feels after the embrace. Did it make you feel calmer or warmer?***

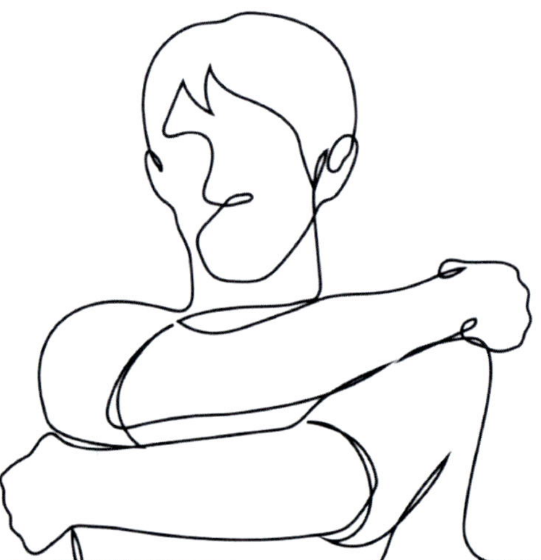

Exercise adapted from "Hugging Practice" exercise developed by Neff K, Germer C. The Mindful Self-Compassion Workbook: A Proven Way to Accept Yourself, Build Inner Strength, and Thrive. The Guilford Press; 2018

☐ *Yes! I tried this exercise*

Time: 5-10 minutes

We all have good qualities that make us unique. We can also think about these good qualities as personal strengths or assets that can be used when we are faced with a problem to solve. Like a suncatcher, our good qualities can also be used to create beams of color that we can share to make our community a better place.

To complete this exercise, think about all the good qualities that make you who you are. Perhaps you are a good listener, are funny, or work well with animals. Write each of these qualities in their own box below. For most people, only a few qualities may come to mind at first. Just like the Nature's Anchor activity, you are invited to use this activity to discover additional parts of yourself that you may forget to appreciate or actively apply during your day. The next time you are faced with a problem, needing some self-compassion, or looking for a way to brighten someone's day, you can look at your suncatcher list below as a reminder of your strengths.

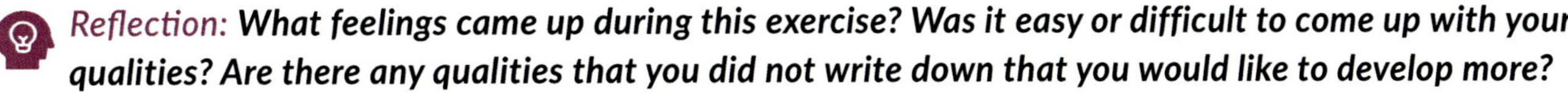

Reflection: ***What feelings came up during this exercise? Was it easy or difficult to come up with your qualities? Are there any qualities that you did not write down that you would like to develop more?***

CREATE YOUR OWN AFFIRMATION

Time: 10 minutes

☐ *Yes! I tried this exercise*

A self-compassion affirmation is something that you say to yourself when you need to practice self compassion and self-love. Use these sayings when stressful or scary things happen to you. The specific words are not important. What is important is that they:

- Come from a place of kindness and acceptance
- Acknowledge that making mistakes and suffering are part of being a human and we all have this in common
- Foster mindful thinking towards negative emotions, meaning you recognize the feeling as it is, not hiding or magnifying it

Pick one phrase from each of one of the boxes below to build your own affirmation. You can use the sayings suggested below or come up with your own.

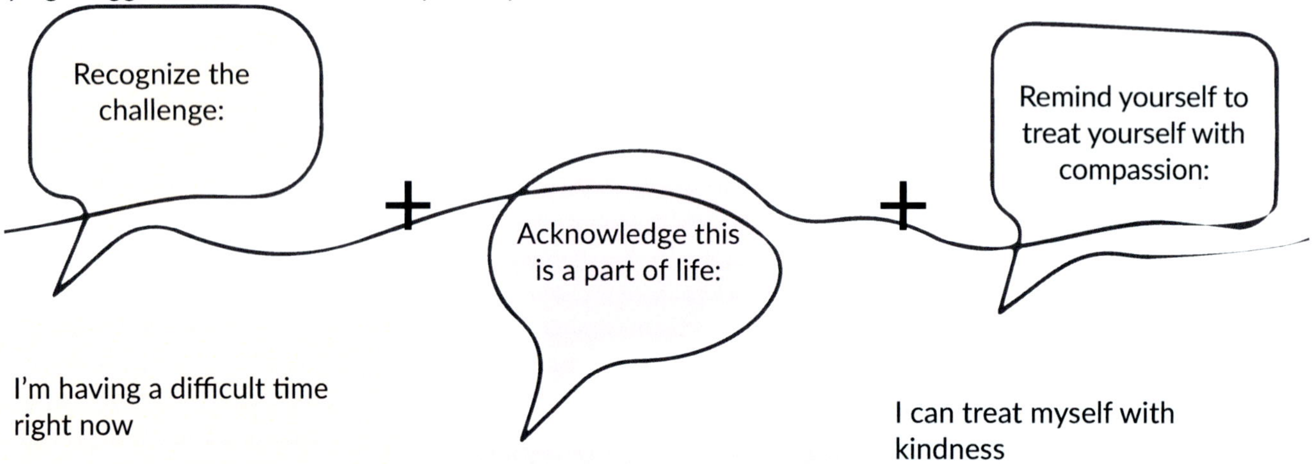

Recognize the challenge: + Acknowledge this is a part of life: + Remind yourself to treat yourself with compassion:

Recognize the challenge:

I'm having a difficult time right now

I'm getting through a temporary rough patch

The road is getting rocky at the moment, but will smooth out soon

Write your own:

____

____

____

____

Acknowledge this is a part of life:

Everyone has times like these

This is part of the human experience

Everyone's life has ups and downs

Write your own:

____

____

____

____

Remind yourself to treat yourself with compassion:

I can treat myself with kindness

I will treat myself like someone I love during this time

I can be gentle to myself

I am deserving of self-compassion

Write your own:

____

____

____

____

Pick three phrases that are the best for you and repeat them until they are memorized. You can also write your affirmation down in a place where you can see it. Use your affirmation the next time you are having a difficult time, or when you begin to judge or talk down to yourself. This is a great way to calm your mind during times of stress.

Exercise adapted from "Developing Your Self-Compassion Mantra" exercise developed by Neff K, Germer C. The Mindful Self-Compassion Workbook: A Proven Way to Accept Yourself, Build Inner Strength, and Thrive. The Guilford Press; 2018

☐ *Yes! I tried this exercise*

 *Time: 1 minute*

Touch can be a powerful tool that we can use to help ourselves feel comforted and secure. We can harness this power by placing one or both of our hands on our physical body in a gentle and caring way. People have different emotional responses to different types of self-touch, so this exercise is about finding what type of physical touch feels truly supportive for you. If you find a gesture that works for you, you can use this to comfort yourself whenever you are under stress.

Try this exercise in a place where you don't have to worry about anyone seeing you. See the list below of some different movements people use to comfort themselves. Try these out and feel free to add some of your own.

» Placing one or both hands on your heart

» Placing one hand on your heart and the other on your belly

» Gently stroking your cheek or arm

» Placing both hands on your belly

» Crossing your arms for a gentle hug

» Gently holding your face with your hands

» Something else:______________________________

____

Sometimes self-touch does not feel comforting or soothing due to memories of past experiences. If this happens to you, try touching something else that is warm or soft, like a blanket, pillow, or pet. The point is to show yourself kindness and love in a way that best fits your needs.

If you find this exercise soothing, try using these physical touches when you feel stressed or upset. If your body feels safe and cared for, your mind and heart will follow easier.

 *Reflection:* ***Did you find a movement that felt comforting to you? Was there anything that surprised you?***

Exercise adapted from "Soothing Touch" exercise developed by Neff K, Germer C. The Mindful Self-Compassion Workbook: A Proven Way to Accept Yourself, Build Inner Strength, and Thrive. The Guilford Press; 2018

SELF-CARE EXERCISES

GRATITUDE

Exercises in this section:

- Appreciation Scavenger Hunt
- Grateful Doodles
- One Grateful Minute
- Gratitude Walk
- Taking Five

Listen to these activities here:

What is gratitude and what does it have to do with food?

The emotions we experience on a daily basis can have a big impact on our overall happiness and well-being. Both negative and positive emotions are a normal part of life. Chronic stress can amplify our experience of negative emotions, like anxiety, depression, and anger. Chronic stress can also drown out our ability to experience and recognize opportunities for positive emotions.

Gratitude has been called the "'gateway" to positive emotions because it can help us find meaningful sources of joy, hope, inspiration, and awe in our daily lives. It is a simple way to connect to ourselves and others by appreciating the good things in our lives.

Like mindfulness, gratitude can be practiced several times throughout the week to help build your positive emotion "muscles." Gratitude can help boost our mood, strengthen our body and immune system, and even improve sleep.

With some awareness and practice, gratitude is something that we can invite into our life just about anytime. Meals and snacks are a great place to start growing your gratitude skills. As you prepare your food and eat, a simple gratitude exercise is to think of all of the unseen work that brought your food to your plate. This section offers a few other exercises that can be done at any time. These exercises can be especially helpful anytime you are feeling bored, lonely, or depressed.

GRATEFUL DOODLES

☐ *Yes! I tried this exercise*

Time: 10 minutes

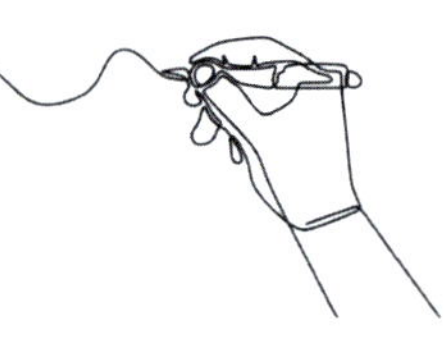

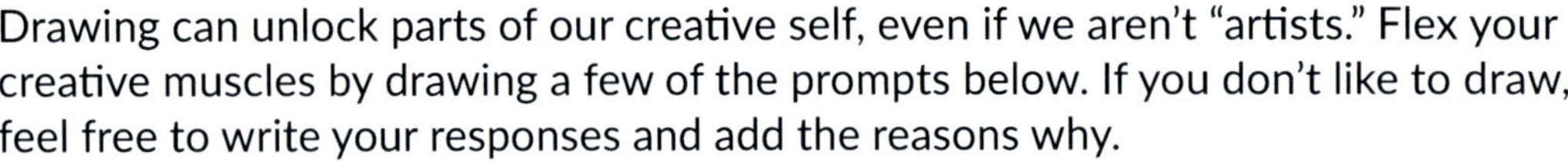

Drawing can unlock parts of our creative self, even if we aren't "artists." Flex your creative muscles by drawing a few of the prompts below. If you don't like to draw, feel free to write your responses and add the reasons why.

Draw something that **makes you happy**.	Draw someone who **helps you.**
Draw something that **makes you smile.**	Draw something you **love to do.**
Draw something you **think is fun.**	Draw something that makes you **feel good.**

[Continues on the next page...]

Draw something that **makes you laugh.**	Draw someone (person or pet) **you love.**
Draw a **meal you eat when you are celebrating.**	Draw your **favorite snack.**

Reflection: ***Which prompts were the easiest to imagine? Which were hard to come up with? Did you notice any patterns in your drawings or responses? Why did you choose the prompts you did?***

ONE GRATEFUL MINUTE

☐ *Yes! I tried this exercise*

 *Time: 1 minute*

Invite one minute into your day that is dedicated to gratitude. During this minute, think of one person who has done something kind for you or has given you some other type of support when you needed it. This person can be anyone from your past or current life, whether it be a friend, teacher, neighbor, family member, healthcare provider, care coordinator, stranger, or even a pet!

To help establish this new habit, try practicing your minute of gratitude right before, during, or immediately after one of your normal daily routines. A good time for recalling this daily dose of gratitude might be while brushing your teeth, taking a shower, or drinking your morning cup of coffee. This practice can also be a nice way to end the day as part of your bedtime routine.

When time allows, you might like to bring this grateful minute further into your day by trying any of the following:

- Send a thank you text message, email, or written card to the person you thought about.
- If the person you thought about can't be reached, think of a way to pass their kindness along to someone else during your day.
- Keep a journal or add scraps of paper to an empty jar to record one line of thanks each day. You could also mark your daily note of gratitude on each square in your monthly calendar. Revisit these later when you are having a difficult day.

Reflection: ***How do my emotions affect my ability to express gratitude to others? How does expressing my gratitude affect my other emotions? How does sharing my gratitude affect others?***

APPRECIATION SCAVENGER HUNT

☐ *Yes! I tried this exercise*

Time: 5 minutes

It's easy to miss the beautiful things around you. This exercise can strengthen your gratitude muscle by slowing down to notice the things that bring you joy.

Look for items (either in nature or around your home) that:

- ☐ Makes you smile
- ☐ Is you favorite color
- ☐ Would make a friend happy
- ☐ Is fun to play with
- ☐ Feels soft to touch
- ☐ Smells good
- ☐ Is beautiful

Reflection: ***Were there any items you had a hard time finding? Did you notice anything new? How did your mood change after you completed your scavenger hunt?***

TAKING FIVE

☐ *Yes! I tried this exercise*

 *Time: 5 minutes*

Make a list of five big things that deeply matter to you that you are thankful for.

This could be people (your partner, your friends, your child, another family member, etc.), a pet, or essential things needed for living, like a place to sleep at night, food to eat, or your clothes.

Make a list of five small, less important things that you may not notice all the time, but that you are grateful for.

This could be a cold glass of water on a summer day, a perfectly ripe piece of fruit, or the smell of garlic cooking.

This exercise can be repeated at the start or end of your day. You don't even need paper: Just use your fingers on each hand to "count your blessings." Taking a few minutes out of your day to be thankful for the big and little things can make a big difference in your mental well-being throughout the day.

Reflection: ***What surprised you about your lists? Which were easier to feel grateful for: Big things or small things? Did you feel different after you completed this exercise?***

Exercise adapted from "Gratitude for the Big and Small Things" exercise developed by Neff K, Germer C. The Mindful Self-Compassion Workbook: A Proven Way to Accept Yourself, Build Inner Strength, and Thrive. The Guilford Press; 2018

☐ *Yes! I tried this exercise*

 *Time: 20+ minutes*

A gratitude walk invites you to experience something that we do every day in a different way. You can experiment with taking a gratitude walk at dawn, mid-day, and dusk. Take note of any differences in how you experience your walk based on the time of day. To start a gratitude walk, simply follow these steps:

1. You may choose to take your gratitude walk alone or with someone else. Choose a time when you don't have to hurry and can take a slow pace. Pick a place that is peaceful to you.
2. Before you begin, consider turning your cell phone off or putting it on silent mode to help remove distractions.
3. Then, take a few full deep breaths and feel your feet rooted to the ground.
4. As you start walking, look around and say to yourself the things you are thankful for. If you are having a hard time getting the words flowing, start with whatever you are thankful for in your physical body, like "I'm thankful for my eyes that can see," or "I'm thankful for my feet." You can also start with things around you, like "I am thankful for the warmth of the sun," or "I'm thankful for the trees." If you are walking with someone else, take turns sharing things you are thankful for.
5. Continue listing things you are thankful for while you walk. If you find yourself running dry, focus on the things right in front of you, "I'm thankful for this path," or "I'm thankful for my shoes."

6. It's okay if you find yourself repeating yourself. If a negative thought comes up, you can say to yourself, "I'm thankful for my ability to recognize negative thoughts and I now release this thought." Then exhale, and continue on your walk.
7. Be creative with your gratitude. You might be surprised what comes up.

If you'd like a slower experience, bring a journal and stop as you are walking, and write down some of the things you are thankful for.

If you have limited mobility, this exercise can be done even if you are in a wheelchair, scooter, or use a cane. This exercise can also be done seated at a park bench while focusing on all of your surroundings.

 *Reflection:* ***Did you notice any changes in how you felt physically or emotionally right after your walk? Was there anything you noticed during your walk that surprised you? If you walked with someone else, how did this affect your experience?***

SELF-CARE EXERCISES

BODY CONNECTION

In this section:

» The Immune System
» The Digestive System

Scan this QR code to follow along with videos:

The immune system is the body's own self-healing mechanism, protecting against germs and other harmful organisms. It maintains the body in a state of regeneration and renewal. The immune system includes the lymphatic system, which includes fluid that travels through vessels in the body and helps you by:

» Moving white blood cells throughout your body to promote healing

» Removing waste products that could damage your cells and organs

» Absorbing and distributing nutrients throughout your body

You might notice swollen areas on your neck when you get sick. Those are lymph nodes (which exist in other parts of the body, too) working hard to fight illness by removing toxins and waste from your body. Unlike the circulatory system, the lymphatic system does not have a pump (heart). It relies on breathing, movement, and gravity to do its work. Practices like deep breathing, hydration, regular movement, and a nutritious diet are crucial for ensuring proper lymphatic flow and your ability to fight off disease.

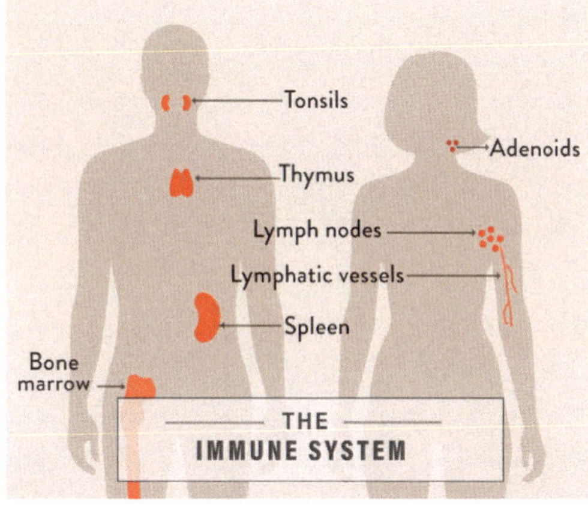

The immune system keeps a record of every germ (microbe) it has ever defeated so it can recognize and destroy the microbe quickly if it enters the body again.

The **immune system** is a complex network of organs, cells, and proteins that defends the body against infection.

Move it: Movement for the immune system

Self-Massage

Use "peace-fingers" over the jaw in front of your ears and massage.

Arm Glides

Extend arm in front with palms touching.

Slide one hand along the other arm as that arm moves to the side. The hand lands at the heart center and then slides back along the arm to meet the other hand in the center.

Side Glides

Bend at the waist while one hand slides down as far as you can reach towards the ankle. The other hand slides all the way up to the armpit.

Switch and bend in the opposite direction. Both palms stay in contact with the body.

The 3 Pillars of Awareness for Moving

Breath

- Notice your breath.
- Rectangle breath through the nose: Inhale. pause. Exhale. pause.

Body

- Line feet up below hips, gently tuck your pelvis, lengthen your lower back
- Lift your heart.
- Lift your shoulders to your ears, roll them back, then drop and relax them down so they are soft.

Eyes

- Soft gaze. Soft breath. Soft body. Soft eyes.

Move it: Movement for the immune system

Bouncing/Jumping

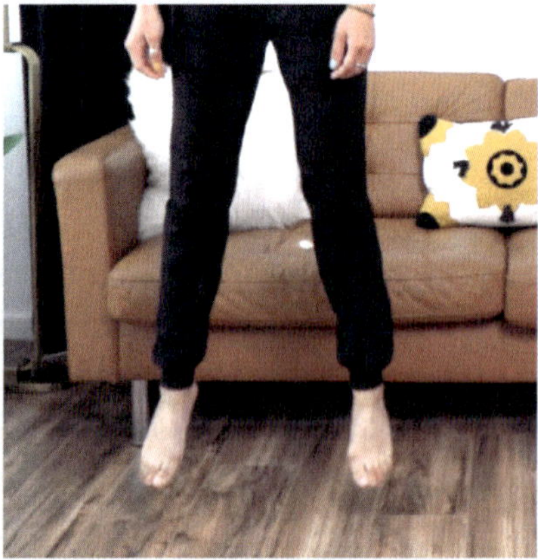

Distribute the weight of the body across the feet and let the upper body bounce (twisting body and arms slightly). First bounce without feet leaving the floor then try jumping

Forward Fold

Seated or standing, elongate the torso with an inhale.

Fold forward at the hips then exhale coming down. Keep hips over the ankles and don't lock your knees.

Let the head and arms hang

Scan this QR code to follow along with videos of this and more connection movements!

Go with the flow

Stay hydrated! Drinking plenty of water supports the movement of vital bodily fluids like blood and lymph, ensuring the delivery of oxygen and nutrients to your cells while removing waste products. Good hydration also helps your body fight illness and disease.

Juicy fruits, soups, and vegetables with high water content also contribute to overall hydration.

Try It! After a long period of walking, standing, or sitting, get some energy back by taking 3 deep breaths and drinking at least 8 oz. of water.

> *"Start where you are. Use what you have. Do what you can."*
>
> —Arthur Ashe, tennis legend

BODY CONNECTION: DIGESTIVE SYSTEM

The digestive system is designed to transform the food you consume into the essential nutrients and energy required for our bodies to survive and thrive. Your digestive, or gastrointestinal (GI) tract, begins at the mouth, where food enters, and ends at the rectum, where the undigested food comes out. It includes the salivary glands, pancreas, liver, stomach, and a long tube known as the intestines.

The gut also hosts a variety of microorganisms (microbiome) that produce many of the chemical messengers your nervous system needs to function optimally. Your digestive system is not only where your body is physically restored but where your mind is, as well. You can think of your gut as your second brain.

Moving your body helps to stimulate your digestive tract helping with the absorption of nutrients, neurotransmitter production, and the maintenance of a healthy gut-brain connection.

Approximately 70-80% of our immune system resides in the gut.

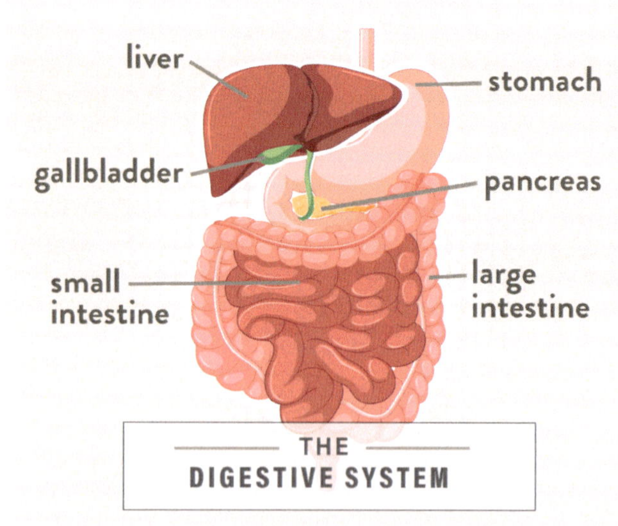

The **digestive system** breaks down food into the nutrients we need to live.

Move it: Movement for the gut

Pelvic Tilt

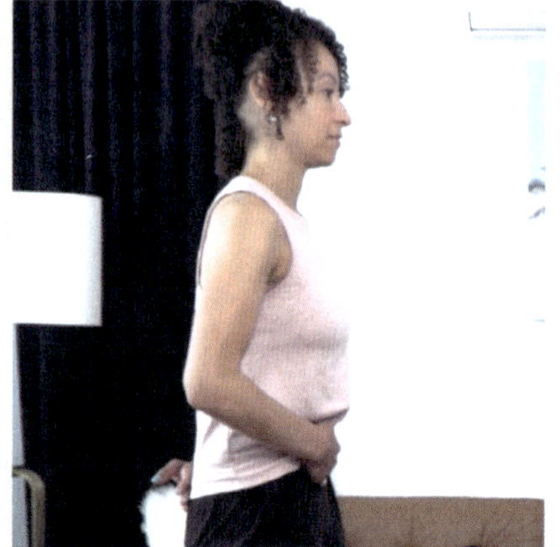

One hand on the belly. one hand on the sacrum.

Keep feet aligned and knees soft.

Tuck the pelvis. Then arch the back. Use a gentle rocking.

Seated Squat

Grasp below the knee and bring up towards the chest. Hold for a few seconds.

Repeat on the other side.

Squat

Feet hip distance apart or slightly wider. Knees are soft.

Drop back as if you are sitting in a chair. Try to keep the body as upright as possible.

Don't let the knees come forward over the toes.

Slowly come down, hold it for just a few seconds. Then slowly come up.

Hold on to a chair if you need extra balance or try the seated squat instead.

The 3 Pillars of Awareness for Moving

Breath

- Notice your breath.
- Rectangle breath through the nose: Inhale. pause. Exhale. pause.

Body

- Line feet up below hips, gently tuck your pelvis, lengthen your lower back
- Lift your heart.
- Lift your shoulders to your ears, roll them back, then drop and relax them down so they are soft.

Eyes

- Soft gaze. Soft breath. Soft body. Soft eyes.

Move it: Movement for the gut

Belly Massage

Place one hand over the other just inside the right hip.

Use the whole palm and apply some pressure.

Slide the hand up along the right side, across the top of the belly, and then down the left side, across the bottom.

Repeat up, across, down, across.

Twist

Seated Twist

Feet stay in place but don't twist so much that the knees are turning in a lot. Twist from the lower spine not the shoulders or neck.

Reach across, back to center.

Exhale on the extension. Inhale as you come to center.

Can be done seated or standing.

Scan this QR code to follow along with videos of this and more connection movements!

Rest and digest

Did you know that your gut acts as a mirror, reflecting the emotions you experience? When your nervous system registers stress, your body may respond by slowing or stopping digestion to redirect all its energy to the **fight-or-flight** stress response. This is why you may feel butterflies in your stomach when speaking in front of an audience or lose your appetite when upset. Conversely, a calm, rested state allows the gastrointestinal tract to focus on digestion and protecting you from potentially harmful substances. Practicing different types of self-care as well as good nutrition for gut health can help you more easily reach this **"rest and digest"** state.

It's normal to crave a favorite treat or snack food during stress, but it's important to be mindful. Ultra-processed foods like sugary drinks, candies, fast food, prepackaged snacks, and frozen desserts can make things worse over time. Artificial additives, stabilizers, excess sugar, and excess salt contribute to a compromised stress response and poor gut health. For a healthier brain and body, try more simple, whole ingredients!

Super Snacks: hummus and veggies, popcorn, low sugar yogurt with fruit, a banana, nuts, or avocado toast

> *"As you breathe in, cherish yourself. As you breathe out, cherish all beings."*
>
> —Dalai Lama

BUNDLES

Looking for some meal ideas? Use this section for some cooking inspiration with these healthy kitchen staples:

» Canned chicken
» Oats
» Lentils
» Tofu
» Dehydrated Vegetables

Canned Chicken

Canned chicken is a lean, ready-to-eat protein option to keep on hand for days when you don't feel like cooking from scratch. A 12-ounce can of chicken only costs a few dollars and has enough protein to feed 4 people.

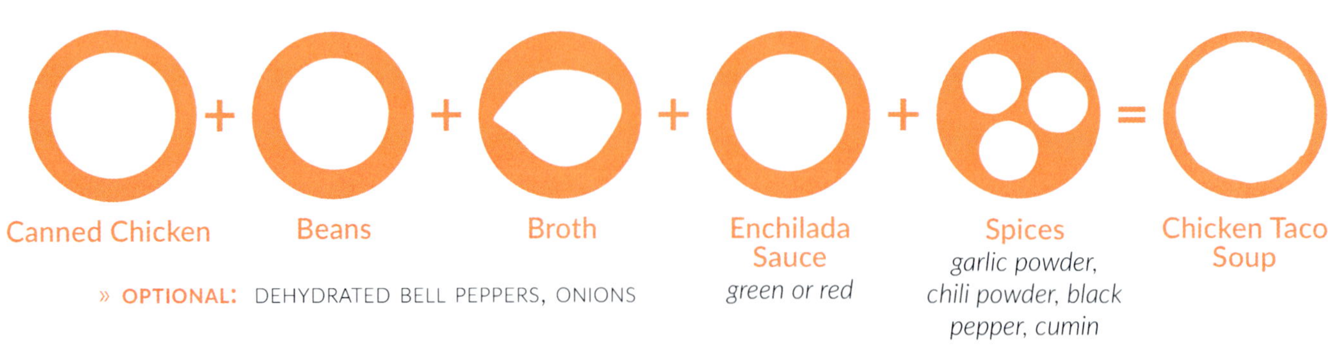

» **OPTIONAL:** DEHYDRATED BELL PEPPERS, ONIONS

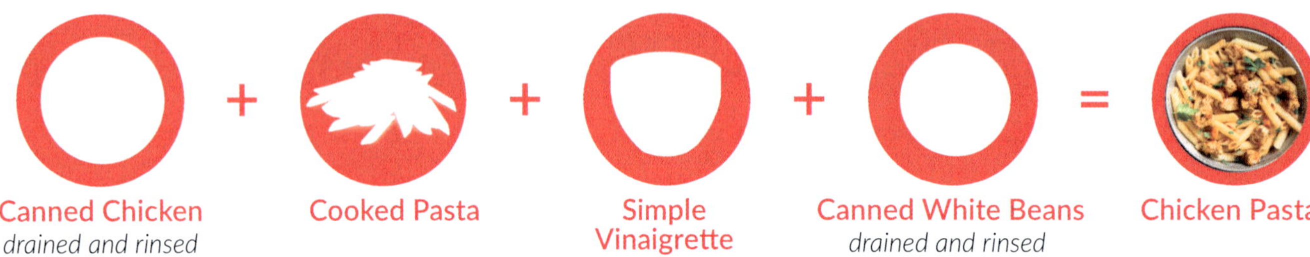

» **OPTIONAL:** CHOPPED VEGETABLES OF YOUR CHOICE

» **OPTIONAL:** CELERY, APPLES, GRAPES, ONION, SLICED ALMONDS OR PECANS

» **OPTIONAL:** SHREDDED CARROTS, DICED APPLES, CELERY, SLICED ALMONDS OR PECANS

» **OPTIONAL:** CANNED BEANS, CANNED TOMATOES (PETITE DICED)

Try It! Create your own canned chicken recipes.

Canned Chicken

Canned Chicken

Canned Chicken

Oats

Oatmeal doesn't have to be boring! This simple ingredient costs less than 25 cents per serving and can be enjoyed both hot and cold. Whether you're craving savory or sweet, you can create a new oat recipe for each day of the week using different combinations of spices, fruits, and even vegetables. Here are a few ideas to help get you started.

Try It! Create your own oatmeal recipes.

Oats

Oats

Oats

LENTILS

Lentils

Lentils are packed with protein and fiber and cost less than 25 cents per serving. Simply rinse dry lentils, place them in a pot of water or broth, and ***simmer*** (cooking at a temperature right below boiling) on the stove for around 25 minutes until they are tender. Here are a few ideas for using lentils in easy and simple ways.

» **DIRECTIONS:** simmer together for 25 minutes

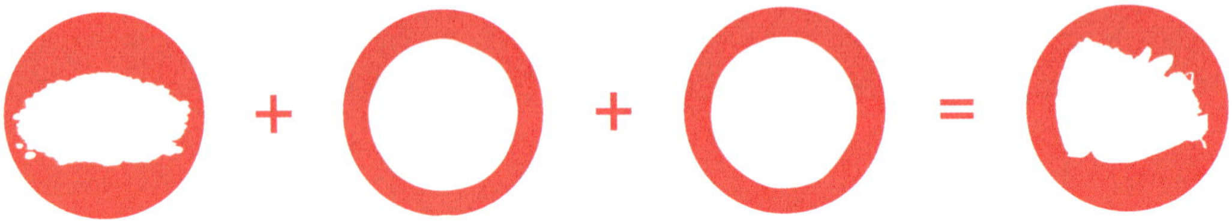

Cooked Lentils + Cumin + Chili Powder = Taco Filling

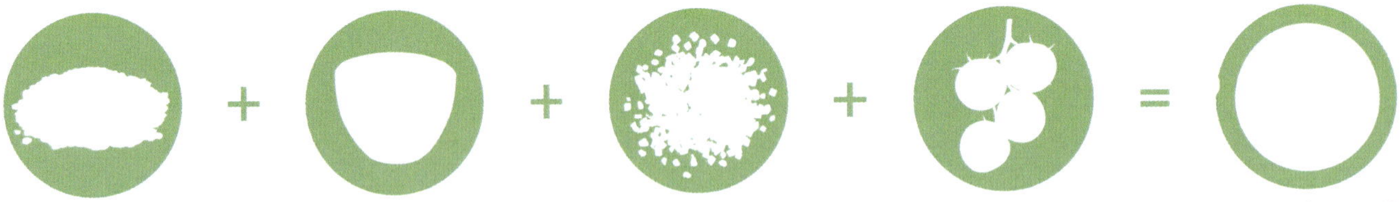

Cooked Lentils + Vinaigrette + Diced Onion + Tomato = Chilled Lentil Salad

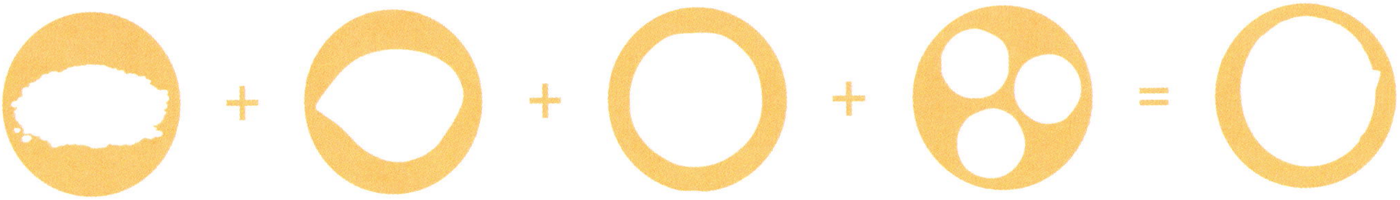

Lentils + Broth + Dried or Fresh Spinach + Spices *cumin, chili powder, garam masala,* = Lentil Daal

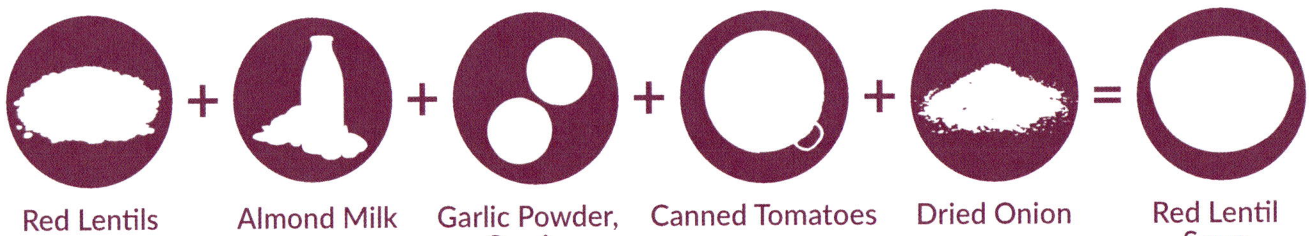

» **OPTIONAL:** ROASTED SWEET POTATOES

Try It! Create your own lentil recipes.

Lentils

Lentils

Lentils

Tofu

Made from soy milk, tofu is created using a process similar to the first steps of making cheese from cow's milk. But unlike cheese, tofu has little to no flavor, so it's up to you to find ways to flavor the tofu with seasonings and other ingredients that you enjoy. Tofu is a great way to beef up the protein in just about any dish. Tofu can be eaten cold or hot and requires no additional cooking.

Tofu + Mustard + Dried Onions + Mayo = Eggless Egg Salad

Tofu: *Mashed or Diced*

» **OPTIONAL:** PICKLE RELISH, CELERY

See "Eggless Egg Salad" recipe for all the details

Tofu + Ramen Noodles + Dried Vegetables = Ramen Tofu

Tofu: *Cube*

» **OPTIONAL:** FRESH VEGETABLES, HARD-BOILED EGG

Tofu + Favorite Dry Dip Mix = Tofu Dip

Tofu + Almond Milk + Fresh or Frozen Berries + Banana = Smoothie

» **OPTIONAL:** PEANUT BUTTER

Tofu + Mayo + Soy Sauce + Dried Onion + Lemon Juice = Tofu Sandwich or Cracker Spread

» **OPTIONAL:** DICED CELERY

Try It! Create your own tofu recipes.

Tofu

Tofu

Tofu

10 WAYS TO BUNDLE WITH DEHYDRATED VEGETABLES

10 ways to use dehydrated vegetables when you don't have fresh or frozen on hand

Dehydrated vegetables are popular among backpackers and campers because they are light to carry and easy to prepare. These foods are also great options in our home kitchen when we don't have the time or the energy to prepare fresh vegetables. They are just as nutritious as fresh and frozen vegetables, too! Only a few tablespoons of dehydrated vegetables per person are needed to make a great meal. Here are a few examples of how to use dehydrated vegetables:

Casserole Filling: Add ½ cup dehydrated vegetables to your favorite breakfast or dinner casserole dish before baking.

Vegetable Stock: Combine ½ cup dried vegetable mix with fresh or dried savory herbs like parsley, sage, thyme, and chives with 2 quarts of water. Simmer for an hour or more.

Overnight Dip: Mix ¼ cup dried vegetables in 1 cup of regular plain or Greek yogurt along with your favorite seasoning like garlic powder or dry or fresh dill. Allow to sit overnight for a delicious dip for sliced raw veggies to eat the next day.

Whole Grain Vegetable Pilaf: Combine quinoa, bulgur wheat, or barley with water according to package directions; stir ½ cup of dried vegetables while cooking. Try also adding dried vegetables to flavored rice mix.

Flavorful Beans: Mix 1 cup of dried vegetables, 1 pound dried beans, 1 Tbsp. reduced sodium bouillon paste, and 7 cups of water with other spices and herbs of your choice. Simmer on the stove or cook in crockpot until beans are done.

Hearty Garden Chili: Add 1 cup of dried vegetable blend to your favorite crockpot chili recipe.

Veggie Spaghetti: Combine 1 jar of spaghetti sauce with ½ cup dehydrated vegetables. Simmer for 15-30 minutes until vegetables are soft before serving.

Instant Soup: Mix ¼ cup of dried vegetables with any instant noodle soup packages.

Crockpot Vegetable Soup: Mix 2 cups of dried vegetables with 1 can low-sodium tomatoes, 4 cups water, and your favorite spices and herbs. Cook on low heat for 1-2hours.

Split Pea or Lentil Soup: Combine 1 pound bag of lentils or split peas, 1 cup dried vegetables, 1 Tbsp. reduced sodium bouillon paste, and 7 cups of water with other spices and herbs of your choice. Simmer on the stove for 30 minutes.

RECIPES

Looking for more meal ideas? Give these nourishing recipes a try:

- Basic Whole Grain Pilaf
- Mexican-style Quinoa or Barley
- Salmon Patties
- Easy Vinaigrette
- Moroccan Carrot Lentil Soup
- Hearty Lentil Chili
- Savory Oat and Lentil Bowl
- Eggless Egg Salad

BASIC WHOLE GRAIN PILAF

Ready In 15+ min. **Serves** 4

A pilaf is a simple recipe that combines whole grains, stock or broth, and spices or seasonings that can be enjoyed as an easy side dish. Looking for a full meal? Simply add vegetables, beans, and/or meat of your choice.

Ingredients

1 tablespoon olive or canola oil
½ onion, finely chopped
2-3 cloves garlic, minced
1 cup intact grain of your choice
water or low-sodium vegetable broth (see table below for amount)
¼ teaspoon kosher salt
Pinch of ground black pepper
Optional: 2-4 Tbsp of dehydrated vegetables of your choice

Directions

1. Heat a medium saucepan over medium high heat.
2. Add oil and heat until shimmering.
3. Add chopped onion and sauté until onions are translucent but not browned.
4. Add garlic and allow to cook until fragrant, about 2 minutes. Do not brown.
5. Add grain and cook until grains are dry or even a bit browned.
6. Add water or stock, optional dehydrated vegetables, and bring to a boil.
7. Reduce heat to low (barely a bubble).
8. Stir in black pepper and place a lid over the pot.
9. Allow to cook on low for the appropriate amount of time per the grain you are using or until grains are tender and liquid is absorbed. If liquid is not absorbed, replace the lid and cook until it is.
10. Remove from heat and allow to rest with the lid on for 5 more minutes.
11. Fluff grain with a fork and serve.

Intact Grain (1 cup)	Liquid	Cook time	Makes
Barley, hulled	3 cups	45-60 minutes	3.5 cups
Barley, pearled	3 cups	25-40 minutes	3.5 cups
Bulgur Wheat	2 cups	10-12 minutes	3 cups
Quinoa	2 cups	15 minutes	3 cups
Steel cut oats	4 cups	20-30 minutes	4 cups

☐ ***Yes! I tried it!***

Other ingredients I used or foods I ate this recipe with to make this meal “mine” (optional):

___

MEXICAN-STYLE QUINOA OR BARLEY

Ready In 30 min. Serves 6

This example pilaf recipe uses vegetable juice to add color, flavor, and extra nutrition to cooked whole grains. Add corn and beans as optional ingredients for a satisfying meal.

Ingredients

1 ½ cups dry quinoa or pearled barley
1 Tbsp. canola oil or olive oil
1 whole white or yellow onion, finely diced
2-3 cloves garlic, crushed, and minced
1 cup low-sodium V8 or vegetable juice
2 cups reduced low-sodium vegetable stock
1 tsp. paprika
¼ tsp. pepper
Optional: Frozen or canned corn, canned beans

Directions

1. Heat a saucepan over medium heat
2. Add 1 tablespoon of oil and heat until shimmering.
3. Add chopped onion and sauté for about 5 minutes, until onions are translucent but not browned.
4. Add garlic and sauté for about 2 minutes, until fragrant.
5. Add low-sodium vegetable juice and quinoa, stir and bring to a boil. If using barley instead of quinoa, add an extra 1 cup of water to pan.
6. Reduce heat to low, cover with a lid and simmer until liquid is absorbed and grain has fully expanded, about 25 minutes (up to 15 minutes longer for barley).
7. Add optional corn and/or beans.
8. Remove from heat and allow to rest 5 minutes. Top with chopped fresh tomato and cilantro, if desired.

☐ ***Yes! I tried it!***

Other ingredients I used or foods I ate this recipe with to make this meal "mine" (optional):

____

____

____

SALMON PATTIES

Ready In 16-20 min. **Serves** 2

These high-protein salmon patties are easy to prepare and are rich in omega 3s to support a healthy mood and heart.

Ingredients

5 ounce pouch salmon
1 tablespoon mayonnaise
1 egg, well beaten
¼ teaspoon ground black pepper
1 teaspoon dehydrated onion
¼ cup finely crushed saltine crackers (or breadcrumbs or panko)
2 Tbsp olive, avocado, or canola oil
1 tsp. paprika
¼ tsp. pepper

Optional:
Frozen or canned corn, canned beans

Directions

1. Combine all ingredients in a small mixing bowl and mix very well. Allow to sit about 10-15 minutes for onions to soften.
2. Divide mixture in half and shape into 2 patties.
3. Heat about 2 tablespoons of olive oil over medium heat in a nonstick pan and add patties. Allow patties to cook until well browned on one side then flip and cook the other side, about 3 minutes on each side.

Serving Suggestions: Enjoy on a bed of greens as a salad with vinaigrette, as a main course with sides of vegetables, on a bun with sriracha mayo as a salmon burger, or in a wrap with greens and veggies with vinaigrette.

☐ ***Yes! I tried it!***
Other ingredients I used or foods I ate this recipe with to make this meal "mine" (optional):

____

____

____

EASY VINAIGRETTE

Ready In 5 min. **Serves** 8

Here is a simple recipe to create your own homemade vinaigrette. Once you've mastered the basic steps, you can try using different acids (like orange juice, balsamic or red wine vinegar) and herbs to create your own unique recipe! This vinaigrette isn't just for salads, enjoy it drizzled over lentils or cooked whole grains, like barley, to infuse these basic foods with big flavor.

Ingredients

¾ cup olive oil
¼ cup lemon juice or apple cider vinegar
2-3 tablespoons water
½ teaspoon salt
¼ teaspoon black pepper

For more flavor, also add:
1 teaspoon garlic powder or 1 teaspoon dehydrated onion
2 teaspoons Dijon mustard
1 teaspoon (or more) dried Italian herb blend

Directions

1. Whisk all ingredients in a bowl with a fork or shake everything together in a lidded jar.
2. Enjoy immediately or store in the refrigerator with a tight fitting lid for up to one week.

☐ ***Yes! I tried it!***

Other ingredients I used or foods I ate this recipe with to make this meal "mine" (optional):

____

____

____

MOROCCAN CARROT LENTIL SOUP

Ready In 35 min. | Serves 8

This red lentil soup offers a quick and easy bowl of warm and comforting "yum"! A delicious blend of cumin, coriander, paprika, cinnamon and turmeric make simple ingredients come alive into a unique, one pot meal.

Ingredients

- 3 Tbsp. olive, avocado, or canola oil
- ½ cup dried mixed vegetables
- ¼ cup dried carrot
- ¼ cup dried onion
- 3 garlic cloves, chopped
- 2 tsp. ground coriander
- 1 tsp. ground cumin
- 1 tsp. ground turmeric
- ½ tsp. sweet paprika
- ¼ tsp. ground cinnamon
- Pinch of red pepper flakes
- Dash of pepper
- 8 cups vegetable broth, low sodium if possible
- 1, 10 oz can petite diced tomatoes
- 2 cups red lentils, washed and rinsed

Optional ingredients:

- 1 lemon, juiced
- 4 Tbsp. fresh flat-leaf parsley, chopped
- 1 Tbsp. fresh cilantro, chopped

Directions

1. Pre-measure all spices and other ingredients before beginning.
2. Heat olive oil in a large pot over medium heat. Add the garlic, coriander, cumin, turmeric, paprika, cinnamon, and pepper and cook for 2-3 minutes stirring the whole time. Turn temperature down if needed to prevent garlic from burning.
3. Add the dried mixed vegetables, dried onions, and dried carrots and stir for another minute.
4. Add the broth, tomatoes, and lentils to the pot. Stir well, turn heat up until soup begins to boil. Then, turn heat down to low and simmer uncovered until the lentils are tender (about 20 minutes), stirring occasionally.
5. For a creamy soup, you can use an immersion blender to make soup smooth right in the pot. For extra flavor, optional ingredients can also be added, including lemon juice, parsley and cilantro (after blending).
6. Cover and cook for 10 more minutes. Serve hot with warm pita bread or bread of your choice. Garnish with extra parsley and cilantro if you desire.

Want to use fresh vegetables? No problem!

Simply replace dried vegetables with the following:

- 1 large onion, chopped
- 1 celery stalk, chopped
- 1 carrot, chopped

☐ ***Yes! I tried it!***

Other ingredients I used or foods I ate this recipe with to make this meal "mine" (optional):

____

HEARTY LENTIL CHILI

Ready In 40 min. Serves 4

This mild, plant-based chili combines simple ingredients with familiar spices to create a savory, high-protein dish. Add extra vegetables or toppings to make this recipe yours!

Ingredients

1 large onion, chopped (or 3 Tablespoons dried)
1 bell pepper, chopped (or 3 Tablespoons dried)
3-5 cloves garlic, minced
1 ¼ cups dried lentils
1 can beans, such as kidney, rinsed and drained
4 cups water or vegetable broth
28 ounces diced canned tomatoes with juice
1 small can tomato sauce
1 ½ teaspoon cumin
2 tablespoons chili powder

Crockpot Directions

1. Plug in crockpot and turn setting to high.
2. Combine all ingredients except canned beans and stir well.
3. Cover crockpot with lid. Leave crockpot on high heat for 4-5 hours or until lentils are tender. Add water or stock if soup becomes too thick while cooking.
4. Once soup is done, stir in canned beans. Allow to rest before serving, about 20 minutes.

Stovetop Directions

1. Combine all ingredients into a large soup pot.
2. Bring to a boil, reduce heat to a simmer, and cook covered for 25 minutes.
3. Uncover and cook for an additional 15 minutes or until chili reaches desired thickness.

☐ ***Yes! I tried it!***

Other ingredients I used or foods I ate this recipe with to make this meal "mine" (optional):

____

____

____

SAVORY OAT AND LENTIL BOWL

Ready In 30-35 min. **Serves** 4

We often think of ways to enjoy oats with sweet ingredients like cinnamon and raisins. But, this simple food can be transformed into a warm, filling, and savory meal that can be enjoyed for breakfast, lunch, or dinner. This recipe adds lentils to the oats while they cook to give them a hearty boost of protein.

Ingredients

¾ cups steel cut oats
4 cups vegetable stock or broth
1 cups dry lentils, picked through and rinsed

Optional:
1 Tablespoon dehydrated onion
2-4 Tablespoons other dehydrated vegetables, such as mixed, bell pepper, or carrots
1 teaspoon curry powder

Directions

1. In a medium saucepan, combine oats, stock, lentils, and optional ingredients (dehydrated vegetables, curry powder).
2. Bring to a boil, reduce to low, cover with a lid and simmer for about 25 minutes or until liquid is absorbed. Taste lentils and oats to check for doneness. Lentils should be soft and oats should be tender. Remove from heat.
3. Allow to rest for 5-10 minutes before serving.

Serving Suggestions: For a simple meal, enjoy anytime "as is" or top with sauteed greens and/or roasted vegetables.

☐ ***Yes! I tried it!***

Other ingredients I used or foods I ate this recipe with to make this meal "mine" (optional):

____

____

____

EGGLESS "EGG" SALAD

Looking for a new way to try tofu? This high-protein recipe is easy to make and can be enjoyed on crackers, raw vegetables, or as a sandwich filling.

Ingredients

1-pound block firm tofu, drained
½ teaspoon salt
1 teaspoon turmeric
⅓ cup mayonnaise
⅓ cup sweet or dill pickle relish
2 tablespoons dehydrated vegetables (your choice) or fresh, diced onion and/or celery
½ teaspoon garlic powder
½ teaspoon onion powder
1 tablespoon Dijon mustard

Directions

1. In a medium-sized bowl, gently mash the tofu, salt, and turmeric until all ingredients are well mixed and there are no large chunks remaining.
2. Add the rest of the ingredients and mix well. Adjust seasonings to taste.
3. If using dehydrated vegetables, allow mixture to chill in the refrigerator for at least one hour before serving.

☐ ***Yes! I tried it!***

Other ingredients I used or foods I ate this recipe with to make this meal "mine" (optional):

____

____

____

EXPLORING THE MEANING OF FOOD IN MY LIFE SURVEY

Have you ever thought about what is important to you about food? Is food something that is important to your life? In what way? What values motivate your food choices the most? Social, sacred, aesthetic, health, or ethical? What are some examples of these values in your life?

Read each statement below and rate it on a scale of 1 to 7.

1 = I strongly disagree

2 = I mostly disagree

3 = I disagree somewhat

4 = I don't agree or disagree

5 = I agree somewhat

6 = I mostly agree

7 = I strongly agree

Add up the totals in each section and divide in order to get your personal rating for each set of values.

Aesthetic: You appreciate the artistry and beauty of good food and the dining experience

_______Preparing a good meal is like making a work of art.

_______A good meal is like a work of art.

_______Eating a good meal is an aesthetic experience like going to a good concert or reading a good novel.

_______I can appreciate the beauty of a dish even if I do not like it.

_______ ÷ 4= _________

Social: You care about how food allows you to interact with and connect to people

_______Food is closely tied to my relationships with others.

_______When I eat I feel connected to the people I am eating with.

_______Food is a way for me to connect with my cultural traditions.

_______Sharing food with others makes me feel closer to them.

_______Making food for others is a main way I show care for them.

_______ ÷ 5= _________

Health: You care about having good nourishment to ensure your physical well-being

_______I get satisfaction from knowing that the food I eat is good for my health.

_______Eating foods that I know are good for my body brings me comfort.

_______I feel that nourishing my body is a meaningful activity.

_______I eat in a way that expresses care for my body.

_______ ÷ 4= _________

[Continues on the next page...]

Sacred: You have spiritual beliefs and a sense of a higher purpose that is reflected in how you eat

_______What I eat is a reflection of my spiritual beliefs.

_______From a spiritual perspective some foods are better than others.

_______My food choices are a way for me to connect with the sacred.

_______Some foods are spiritually polluting.

_______ ÷ 4 = _________

Ethical: You are concerned with doing the right thing for society, animals or the environment when it comes to food.

_______ I care about the impact of my food choice on the world.

_______My food choices are an important way that I can affect the world.

_______When I eat food I think about where it came from.

_______I eat in a way that expresses care for the world.

_______My food choices reflect my connection to nature.

_______ ÷ 5= _________

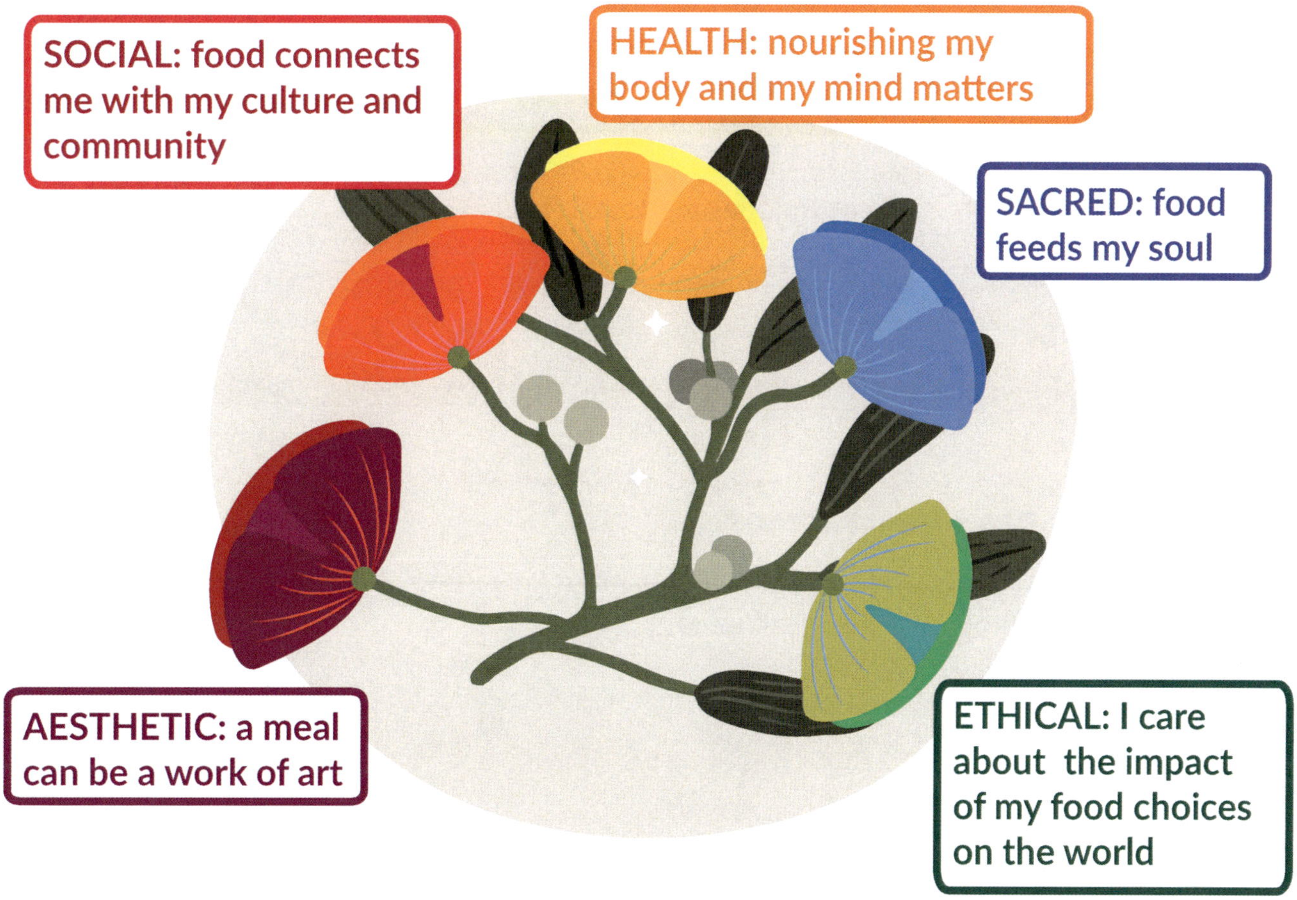

SOCIAL: food connects me with my culture and community

HEALTH: nourishing my body and my mind matters

SACRED: food feeds my soul

AESTHETIC: a meal can be a work of art

ETHICAL: I care about the impact of my food choices on the world

Arbit, N., Ruby, M., Rozin, P., Development and validation of the meaning of food in life questionnaire (MFLQ): Evidence for a new construct to explain eating behavior. Food Quality and Preference. 2017;59:35-45. https://doi.org/10.1016/j.foodqual.2017.02.002.

REFERENCES

Week 1

Arbit, N., Ruby, M., Rozin, P., Development and validation of the meaning of food in life questionnaire (MFLQ): Evidence for a new construct to explain eating behavior. Food Quality and Preference. 2017;59:35-45. https://doi.org/10.1016/j.foodqual.2017.02.002.

Week 2

Center for Mind-Body Medicine. Self-care Basics: Mindful Eating. https://cmbm.org/self-care-basics/

Week 5

Curio Spice. Story of the Spice Wheel. Curio Spice Blog. Published September 8, 2023. Accessed February 13th, 2024. https://curiospice.com/blogs/curio-spice-blog/story-of-the-spice-wheel

Week 7

Grubinger, V. With an Ear to the Ground: Essays on Sustainable Agriculture. NE Region Sustainable Agriculture Research & Ed.; 2004

Week 10

The Hunger-Satiety Scale. University Health Services Berkeley. Accessed May 8, 2024. https://uhs.berkeley.edu/sites/default/files/wellness-hungersatietyscale.pdf.

Self-Care Exercises

Dragonfly Tea. How to Press Pause with a Little 'Tea Mindfulness'. Dragonfly Tea Blog. Published October 12, 2021. Accessed March 4, 2024. https://dragonflytea.com/blogs/our-blog/tea-mindfulness

Neff, K. D. Development and validation of a scale to measure self-compassion. Self and Identity. 2003; 2: 223-250. DOI:10.1080/15298860390209035

Neff K, Germer C. The Mindful Self-Compassion Workbook: A Proven Way to Accept Yourself, Build Inner Strength, and Thrive. The Guilford Press; 2018

Made in the USA
Middletown, DE
20 June 2024

56100249R10115